"Like Aaron Copland in his classic *What to* [...] tholomew helps readers of the Bible to know [...] [...] in Scripture and how to do so with attention and intelligence, in spirit and in truth. Bartholomew uses both ears, the academic and the devotional, and three hermeneutics (liturgical, ethical, and missional) to listen especially to what is most important: God's address, words that guide and govern the church today."

—**Kevin J. Vanhoozer**, Trinity Evangelical Divinity School

"*Listening to Scripture* is remarkably expansive and accessible in its vision and applicability as it guides Christians through an integrative journey of personal devotions, academic study, preaching and teaching, and missional outreach. I am already incorporating the book's insights and devotional exercises into my own life, my undergraduate Old Testament classes, and my parish Bible study. *Listening to Scripture* is the integrative vision that I have been hungering for and that my students and fellow congregants so desperately need. Its vision and invitation encompass the wholeness of our being so that God's work of redemption flows into us and through us."

—**Megan C. Roberts**, Prairie College

"Craig Bartholomew continues his important project of relocating a post-Enlightenment scientific hermeneutical approach to Scripture within the broader framework of listening to God's address. His earlier book on the issue was outstanding, but its length and academic depth proved challenging to many. In this new book, Bartholomew gives us a shorter and more accessible study that will be suitable for hermeneutics classes in seminaries. I plan to use it in my course. Devotional and warm, *Listening to Scripture* is also rigorous and challenging! A delightful book."

—**Michael W. Goheen**, Missional Training Center, Phoenix, Arizona

"No one has taught me more about reading Scripture seriously as both an academic and a committed Christian than Craig Bartholomew. This accessible introduction to reading the Bible is needed in a time when, as Craig describes it, 'Bibles may be selling like hotcakes, and we may have several in our homes, but that does not necessarily mean a lot of listening and obeying is going on.' While I—and you—may not agree with all of Craig's methods or conclusions, this book is without a doubt an excellent primer for hearing the voice of our triune God in the text of Holy Scripture."

—**Matthew Y. Emerson**, Oklahoma Baptist University

"Once again, Craig Bartholomew delivers a must-read treatise on how to read the Scriptures. As he says, his aim is that we will read the Bible in such a way that it 'sets us running along God's ways in God's world, feeling his pleasure.' Suffice it to say that this book hits where it aims. Bartholomew reminds us that interpreting the Bible must not be divided into 'devotional' versus 'academic' activities. Rather, both head and heart remain engaged, founded on the fear of the Lord, beginning with prayer, and ending with internalizing Scripture so that it becomes part of us, part of our way of being in God's world. Bartholomew calls his readers to consider the historical, literary, and theological dimensions—a triadic approach—and he leads readers to respond liturgically, ethically, and missionally. For such is the broad task of biblical interpretation. This is not just another classroom manual on hermeneutics. It's an exercise in hearing and joyfully obeying the voice of the living God."

—**Benjamin T. Quinn**, Southeastern Baptist Theological Seminary and BibleMesh

Listening
to Scripture

Listening to Scripture

AN INTRODUCTION TO
INTERPRETING THE BIBLE

Craig G. Bartholomew

Baker Academic
a division of Baker Publishing Group
Grand Rapids, Michigan

© 2023 by Craig G. Bartholomew

Published by Baker Academic
a division of Baker Publishing Group
Grand Rapids, Michigan
www.bakeracademic.com

Printed in the United States of America

Library of Congress Cataloging-in-Publication Data
Names: Bartholomew, Craig G., 1961– author.
Title: Listening to scripture : an introduction to interpreting the Bible / Craig G. Bartholomew.
Description: Grand Rapids, Michigan : Baker Academic, a division of Baker Publishing Group, [2023] | Includes bibliographical references and index.
Identifiers: LCCN 2023002262 | ISBN 9780801099038 (paperback) | ISBN 9781540966421 (casebound) | ISBN 9781493437856 (ebook) | ISBN 9781493437863 (pdf)
Subjects: LCSH: Bible—Hermeneutics—Textbooks.
Classification: LCC BS476 .B382 2023 | DDC 220.601—dc23/eng/20230419
LC record available at https://lccn.loc.gov/2023002262

Baker Publishing Group publications use paper produced from sustainable forestry practices and post-consumer waste whenever possible.

23   24   25   26   27   28   29   7 6 5 4 3 2 1

To the trustees and staff of the Kirby Laing Centre for Public Theology in Cambridge. Your support and vision are a great encouragement on our journey.

CONTENTS

PREFACE

If, as Paul says in Ephesians, we are to "learn the Messiah" (Eph. 4:20 AT)—namely, Jesus—then few things are as important as knowing how to read the Bible so that this is most likely to take place. The aim of biblical hermeneutics is precisely to equip us in this respect.

For many years I have worked on biblical hermeneutics, an exhilarating task. Links to many of the publications I have been involved in can be found on the website of the Kirby Laing Centre, of which I am the director: kirbylaingcentre.co.uk.

I am grateful to Jim Kinney and his team at Baker Academic for the kind invitation to write this book. While some academics frown on writing such introductory books, to me they are very important and often far more formative than our academic tomes. My thinking has continued to develop while writing this book, and my prayer and hope are that it will help readers to (re)discover the Bible for what it is—God's Word.

Pronouns, including for God, are a hot topic today. In line with the Bible and most of the theological tradition, I refer to God with "he" and "his" throughout, while recognizing that God transcends gender and is neither male nor female in the way that we are as creatures.

This book will have succeeded if it takes its reader ever more deeply into the Bible itself and thus ever more deeply into the very life of God—Father, Son, and Holy Spirit.

1

RUNNING THE WAY OF
GOD'S INSTRUCTION

Psalm 119:32 has a wonderful image of running along the way of God's commands because God has enlarged our hearts: "I run in the path of your commands, for you have broadened my understanding [Hebrew: my heart]." Years ago an extraordinary film was produced on the life of Eric Liddell, called *Chariots of Fire*. It remains a must-see film. Liddell was an Olympic gold medalist and later a missionary to China. In the film he explains to his sister why he must compete as an athlete: "When I run, I feel [God's] pleasure."[1] Similarly, when our hearts are enlarged and run in the way of God's instruction, like Liddell, we feel God's pleasure.

Of course, it is above all in the Bible that we find *God's* commands, and when we read the Bible, we need to take off our shoes, as it were, because we are on holy ground. We take up the Bible to read it, only to find that through it God speaks to us. This is the awesome potential of Bible reading and interpretation. Read correctly under the influence of the Spirit, the Bible becomes alive, expands our hearts, and sets us running along God's ways in God's world, feeling his pleasure.

1. *Chariots of Fire*, directed by Hugh Hudson, written by Colin Welland, produced by David Puttnam (1981; Burbank, CA: Warner Home Video, 2005).

The aim of this book is to explore how to read and study the Bible so that we are most likely to experience it in this way, the way of abundance rather than of famine.

A Famine of Hearing the Word?

In the West we are spoiled with a plethora of English translations of the Bible. Indeed, the Bible remains the bestseller of all times. I can still recall the excitement—many years ago—of my high school friends and me when the New International Version (NIV) first came out, the version of the Bible used in this book. Since then, many more translations have appeared, as well as dozens of study Bibles and niche market Bibles. We would seem to be in a very different position from the judgment prophesied by Amos to the Northern Kingdom of Israel in the Old Testament:

> "The days are coming," declares the Sovereign LORD,
>   "when I will send a famine through the land—
> not a famine of food or a thirst for water,
>   but *a famine of hearing the words of the* LORD.
> People will stagger from sea to sea
>   and wander from north to east,
> searching for the word of the LORD,
>   but they will not find it." (Amos 8:11–12, emphasis added)

Very few of us in the West have experienced famine. It is a horrific experience as the food and water people depend on are steadily depleted until there is nothing left, and they slowly and painfully die. It is hard to think of a worse experience. For Amos, however, there is indeed a worse experience, and that is to be cut off from God's life-giving Word. Amos understood that we are made for relationship with God, and our well-being depends on that relationship being maintained and nurtured. Because God is God and we are (sinful) creatures, the initiative in this relationship has to come from God and, in particular, from God speaking to us so that we can respond and be drawn ever more deeply into relationship with him.

In Amos's time God's people did not have Bibles as do we. It would be many centuries before the printing press would be invented, so even though much of the Pentateuch—the first five books of the Bible—was written and held in the temple, it would have been impossible to have a personal copy that you could carry around with you. God's people were dependent on the priests to teach them the Torah, as well as on prophets like Amos to bring God's Word to them in their particular historical and cultural context. The famine that Amos has in mind is in particular one of prophecy, and indeed, from the end of the Old Testament until we hear the voice of John the Baptist at the start of the New Testament, there are some four hundred years of silence, during which prophecy was no longer heard in Israel.

Notice that what Amos predicts is a famine of *hearing* the word of the Lord. Hearing includes listening and obeying. This indicates the appropriate human response to God speaking. It also makes us aware of a very real danger in our own time: Bibles may be selling like hotcakes, and we may have several in our homes, but that does not necessarily mean a lot of listening and obeying is going on. There are all sorts of reasons for this, but one is that many people who do long to listen and obey have never been taught *how* to do so.

Avoiding Famine: Psalm 119

Paul observes in Romans 3:2 that it was the great privilege of God's Old Testament people to be "entrusted with the very words of God." Psalm 119 is the longest psalm, and it celebrates the richness and indispensability of God's Word (torah/law, which is more accurately rendered "instruction") for his people, thereby enabling us to see why it is so catastrophic to suffer from a famine of hearing the word of the Lord and how to avoid it. Westermann says, "Psalm 119 is often also considered a wisdom psalm. But what it contains is not really wisdom speech but *a great doxology of God's Word*, of the law of God as it is called most often in this psalm."[2]

Like Psalm 1, Psalm 119 begins with the word *blessed*, as do the Beatitudes of Jesus in Matthew 5. In Psalm 119:12, the psalmist declares YHWH—the most common name for God in the Old Testament, normally translated as "LORD"—"blessed." Psalm 119 is also closely connected through its vocabulary and theme with Psalm 19, which celebrates God's law given at Sinai and his order for the creation, with the former mirroring the latter. *Blessed* thus evokes the idea of a human life upon which God's favor and approval

2. Claus Westermann, *The Psalms: Structure, Content, and Message*, trans. Ralph D. Gehrke (Minneapolis: Augsburg, 1980), 117. Emphasis added.

rest in all its God-given dimensions, which as a result is fully human and free in the very best sense of these words. It is human life sharing in God's own blessedness. The early church father Irenaeus captured this beautifully in his assertion that is commonly rendered, "the glory of God is the human person fully alive."[3]

This should stir a deep longing within us. The question, of course, is how to become such a blessed person. Psalm 119's answer is through God's Word, through his instruction. Mays captures the vision of Psalm 119 succinctly: "*God is the teacher* (vv. 33–39). Creation is the classroom (vv. 89–91, 73). The students are the servants of God (vv. 17, 23, 124f.). The lesson is the 'law' of God (vv. 97–100). Learning is the way of life (vv. 9–16)."[4]

The logic is impeccable. God is the great Creator and therefore knows better than anyone the ways for human and nonhuman life to flourish. To use a common example, imagine you buy a new home gadget and can't figure out how to put it together or use it. Then a friend wisely—perhaps smugly—asks, "Have you read the instructions?" No one knows better how something works than its designer, and it is the same with us and the rest of creation. God is perfect and good, his ways are perfect and good, and for us to flourish we need his instructions.

Of course, God's Word and instructions are no ordinary instructions. Psalm 119:96 says this well: "To all perfection I see a limit, but your commands are boundless." Imagine perfection without limits. That is God. He is perfectly good, perfectly holy, perfectly loving, perfectly powerful, perfectly knowing, and so on. Imagine being taught by such a teacher. You can begin to see why it is so catastrophic for Israel to suffer from a famine of hearing the Word of this God.

Psalm 119 captures the perfection of God's Word not only through its content but also through its form. It is a literary masterpiece. Its form is that of an acrostic poem, with each new section beginning with a letter of the Hebrew alphabet from "A to Z." There are twenty-two sections because there are twenty-two Hebrew letters. Every line in each section begins with the same letter of that section. There is more: just as there are eight lines in each section, so there is a common vocabulary of eight words—translated by the NIV as "law(s)," "statutes," "precepts," "decrees,"

---

3. Irenaeus, *Against Heresies* 4.20.7.
4. James L. Mays, *Psalms*, Interpretation: A Bible Commentary for Teaching and Preaching (Louisville: Westminster John Knox, 1994), 381.

"commands," "word(s)," "promise(s)"—one of which occurs in almost every line of the psalm. Mays comments: "Apparently the poet knew of eight principal terms in the authoritative tradition that named the subject about which he wanted to write. So he used the alphabet to signal completeness and the whole vocabulary to represent comprehensiveness."[5] God's instruction is perfect, because it comes from God: "That is really what is at stake in the thematic vocabulary. All the terms turn on *divine communication*. The unfailing repetition of the possessive pronoun 'your' with every occurrence of the terms emphasizes with an unwearied insistence that what matters is God's use of these modes of language as divine communication."[6] The form of Psalm 119 thus highlights the perfection of God's Word in terms of both its content and its comprehensive range across the whole of life. God speaks, and we live not by bread alone but by every word that God speaks.

Running into Life

Humans have always needed God's instruction in order to flourish. Even the first couple, Adam and Eve, received basic instruction from God for how to live if they were to flourish as his image bearers. As we know, they disobeyed this instruction, with catastrophic consequences for all of us and the whole creation. As their heirs, although we remain God's image bearers, we have our own sin and brokenness that prevent us from hearing and obeying God's Word. In a context in which the world, the flesh, and the devil abound, it is no easy thing to attend to God's Word. Psalm 119 is clearly aware of the many obstacles that get in the way of running along the path of God's instruction: the struggle for a young person to remain pure (v. 9), the experiences of slander (v. 23), disgrace (v. 39), suffering (vv. 50, 75, 86), and more are all clearly in view. In such a world we need God's help with our ears, eyes, and heart so that we can run along his ways with joy.

Too often we, like the Israelites Amos addressed, are hard of hearing. We need God's help to solve this problem, and intriguingly in Psalm 40:6 the psalmist writes, "But my ears you have opened." Literally, the Hebrew reads, "You have dug out my ears!" It is as though we have lost our ears altogether and are therefore unable to hear, but God has restored ears to us and enabled us to hear again. God's Word is rich and life-giving, but

---

5. Mays, *Psalms*, 382.
6. Mays, *Psalms*, 383. Emphasis added.

too often we cannot hear, we cannot see. Thus, we need to pray with the psalmist, "Open my eyes that I may see wonderful things in your law" (Ps. 119:18). To receive God's Word, we need open ears and open eyes.

Each year I normally spend at least a month in my homeland, South Africa. During that time I do a lot of running around the many hills where my family home is located. If I am unfit, then the early runs are difficult. Eventually, however, I reach the stage where I can just run, moments of sheer exhilaration. Psalm 119 anticipates a similar development in our response to God's Word: "I run in the path of your commands, for you have broadened my understanding" (v. 32). In the Hebrew the latter phrase reads, "For you have expanded my heart." In the Old Testament, the heart is the center of a person's existence, out of which flow thoughts, will, and emotions. In order to respond to God's Word, we need an expanded, capacious heart.

The French, Catholic philosopher Jean-Louis Chrétien has a wonderful chapter just on this verse (Ps. 119:32). He notes that "the heart that is dilated, expanded, made capacious thanks to divine action is at the opposite pole of the heart of the proud, which is puffed up, bloated, and self-saturated: 'Their heart is as thick as grease' (v. 69, Bible of Jerusalem)."[7] The dilated heart transforms us and our view of the world. Paradoxically, the heart is expanded *as* it receives God's Word: "The heart, which is the headquarters, biblically speaking, of both intellect and volition, becomes the receptacle of the divine presence when God's Word is understood and put into practice. When the heart is set free, when it is set at large of every shore, everything is vast. When a person runs freely on the way of God's commandments, the way is wide—the same road that seems narrow when we stumble along it, oppressed and unwilling."[8]

Biblical interpretation, understood here as receiving God's Word, requires open ears and eyes and a capacious heart. Where, we might well ask, shall these be found? The answer is, of course, from God. Our eyes and ears are opened and our heart expanded when the Spirit does his regenerative work in us as we respond to the good news of Jesus. Many can testify to the dramatic change they experienced in reading the Bible once they were converted. Conversion, however, is only the beginning. Along

7. Jean-Louis Chrétien, *Spacious Joy: An Essay in Phenomenology and Literature*, trans. Anne Ashley Davenport (New York: Rowman & Littlefield, 2019), 63.
8. Chrétien, *Spacious Joy*, 69.

the journey that follows, again and again we will need our eyes opened, our ears unblocked, and our hearts expanded.

If the goal or telos of biblical interpretation is to listen for God's address, then it must begin and end with God. It must begin in prayer with profound dependence upon God and end in hearing and responding to God's speaking. Mays says of Psalm 119, "The poem is meant to be read aloud to others or to oneself so that the repetitions guide the hearing and the variations enchant the imagination. It establishes a focus of contemplation and evokes the mood of concentration and submission in which meditation occurs."[9]

God's Word comes from God, but for it to be genuinely heard it has to become part of us. It has to be ingested, to be thoroughly internalized until, in George Steiner's evocative words, it becomes the pacemaker of our consciousness.[10] And it has to be obeyed. Paul captures this in his phrase "the obedience of faith" (Rom. 1:5; 16:26 NRSV). Such is the nature of God's Word that it is only as it is received, internalized, and practiced that our hearts are enlarged and our understanding increased. An important way in which we learn that the Bible is truly God's Word is by living it.

Open Heart, Open Mind

Clearly from what we have discussed, the Bible should not be approached neutrally but on our knees with our ears wide open, ready to hear God's address. However, it is possible that you are reading this book as part of a course on biblical interpretation or hermeneutics. In such a course you will be introduced to the academic study of the Bible, learning about the original languages of the Bible (Hebrew, Aramaic, and Greek), literary analysis, historical and cultural background, and much more. Such study is invaluable, but how does it relate to the devotional approach to the Bible mapped out above? Few questions are more important for the serious student of the Bible today.

Let me begin with two wrong answers to this question. The first is the quintessentially modern way—namely, that a devotional reading of the Bible and an academic one are two different things and should be kept quite apart from one another. In a devotional reading, faith is fully engaged, whereas an academic reading is scientific, and reason and objectivity should reign

9. Mays, *Psalms*, 382.
10. George Steiner, *Real Presences* (London: Faber & Faber, 1989), 9.

supreme. This approach is characteristically modern because it bifurcates biblical interpretation along the lines of modernity's privatization of religion. Modernity sought to keep religion out of the great public spheres of life, such as politics, economics, and education, while allowing for freedom of religion within the private aspects of life. From this perspective people can read the Bible devotionally in their private lives and in church, but in education the Bible must be studied "scientifically"—that is, rationally and objectively apart from faith.

The problem is that biblical faith cannot be reduced to private life; it relates to all of life as God has made it, just as does God, the object of faith. Furthermore, the modern narrative that keeping faith out of education makes education objective and neutral is simply not true. One set of commitments is simply exchanged for another, and a tension—often generating a crisis of faith—develops between the two.

The second wrong approach is to collapse devotional and academic readings of the Bible into each other, as if careful parsing of Hebrew and Greek words, detailed study of ancient Near Eastern culture, analysis of the literary structure of a passage or book, or reading a commentary are essentially the same as the receptive, open-hearted nature of devotional reading. A person consistently pursuing this approach ends up doing commentary-type work during devotions and sometimes turns academic study into a sermon or church Bible study. In the process, both types of reading suffer: devotional reading becomes arid and dry, and academic study loses its rigor. The two approaches are different, and we ought not to collapse the one into the other.

However, these approaches are intimately related. I would put it this way: in devotional reading of the Bible, whether individually or in church, the heart dominates while the head remains engaged. In academic biblical study, the head dominates while the heart remains—or should remain—engaged. Historically, the church has always valued both, and we need both, but we need them healthily related to one another. Alas, it is too common for churches to see little value in hard, academic biblical study, and it is also common for biblical scholars to be dismissive of the church. It ought not to be so.

Devotional reading of the Bible goes under different names. In evangelical circles it is common to situate it in the "quiet time," delightfully named as a time apart with God, with the Bible at its heart. Within the Catholic tradition a devotional reading is often referred to as *lectio divina* or spiritual reading. The aim of the latter is to receive God's Word into the heart. This type of reading is sometimes compared to rolling one's tongue over a piece of hard candy, slowly absorbing its flavors. In an Ignatian reading of the Bible,[11] one is encouraged to engage the imagination fully—for example, by entering a biblical narrative as one of the characters and trying to review the scene through that character's eyes.

Listening to preaching is another form of a devotional reception of the Bible. Sometimes one hears sermons that attempt to deepen the teaching ministry of the church by turning the sermon into a lecture. In my view this denatures the sermon. The sermon announces the good news of the Bible under the power of the Spirit and thereby ushers us into the presence of God.

If I had to privilege one approach, I would privilege devotional reading because it specializes in receiving the Bible as what it is: God's Word, his address to us in our hearts. The primary place for the reception of the Bible is the community, the church, gathered with open ears and eyes, ready to attend to what God is saying to his people through his Word. In the order of priority, academic study of the Bible is a secondary but no less dispensable activity that, when done well, deepens our understanding of the Bible immeasurably. Consider this illustration. Think of World War II. The frontline soldiers are where the battle rages. This is like the primary reception of the Bible as God's Word. However, far away in a small British town called Bletchley, a group of scientists are working day and night to break the Enigma code. These scientists are like biblical scholars, working on myriad details of biblical study. Both groups were essential to the Allied victory in the war; their roles were different but complementary.

It is sometimes said that objective, scientific study provides a corrective to interpretation of the Bible informed by faith. This misconstrues the relationship. Both devotional reading and academic analysis should proceed out of faith and to faith, and both can and should be correctives to each other.

How then do you study the Bible in a way that deepens your faith? How can biblical studies help you become more excited about the Bible as God's Word? These are critical questions. At its best, biblical studies is a great

11. That is, the tradition of Ignatius of Loyola (1491–1556).

gift, but there are ways of studying the Bible that leave faith jaded and insecure, if not shipwrecked. Sometimes naïve, simplistic faith *needs* to be challenged in order for it to mature. However, it is not at all uncommon for biblical studies to be conducted in ways designed to undermine faith. The school that resolves any difficult issue with quick references to the Bible's inerrancy and infallibility—vital as these doctrines are—and the school that considers neutral, rational analysis of the Bible the privileged route to truth are both problematic. The ideal place to study the Bible is in a school that honors faith, operates out of it, and is committed to the most rigorous study of the Bible—including the original languages—all in the service of hearing what God is saying.

Finally, as you will often hear on the London Underground, mind the gap, referring to a gap between the train and the platform. Academic study can be so exhilarating that you can begin thinking that the higher your grades are, the more spiritual you have become. This is a fatal mistake, opening up a gap between devotional reading and academic analysis of the Bible. An educational institution is primarily concerned with the formation of the mind. It is not responsible for the state of your devotional life, although it may and should help in this regard. Your devotional reception of the Bible needs to grow and keep pace with your academic study, and you must always make sure that the latter serves your reception of the Bible as God's Word.

This leads us to an important question: How can we do academic study of the Bible such that it serves rather than subverts faith? *Hermeneutics*—a funny word if you have never heard it before—can help.

The Role of Hermeneutics

Not only do we *not* want to experience a famine of God's Word, but positively we want to experience the Bible like the early Christians did. In his wonderful book *The Spirit of Early Christian Thought*, church historian Robert Louis Wilken says of the early Christians, "When they took the Bible in hand they were overwhelmed. It came upon them like a torrent leaping down the side of a mountain."[12] "The Bible," writes Wilken, "formed Christians into a people and gave them a language."[13]

12. Robert Louis Wilken, *The Spirit of Early Christian Thought: Seeking the Face of God* (New Haven: Yale University Press, 2003), 53.
13. Wilken, *Spirit of Early Christian Thought*, 52.

When I was studying theology at Oxford University, I read articles by heroes of mine, like the late J. I. Packer, whom I continue to revere. I remember reading an article by Packer on the inerrancy of the Bible. I found his argument logically compelling, but afterward I was somewhat bemused. Yes, I believed that the Bible is God's fully trustworthy Word, but believing this did not help me know how to study it so that my studies deepened my sense of the Bible as God's living Word. Packer helped me know *what* the Bible is, but less so *how* to study it so as to listen to it so as to hear God speaking to me. It is when we learn how to listen to the Bible that it starts to come alive to us like a torrent leaping down a mountain.

Hermeneutics is a scary, big word. When the word first became fashionable in Christian circles in the late twentieth century, some joked that Herman Neutics was the name of a German theologian! However, there is no need to be scared of hermeneutics. It comes from the Greek word *hermēneuō*, meaning to explain, expound, translate, or interpret. In the second half of the twentieth century, philosophical hermeneutics developed in a major way, particularly through the work of Hans-Georg Gadamer (1900–2002) in his magisterial work *Truth and Method*. In this work Gadamer focuses on how we go about understanding, for example, an artwork. For our purposes, *biblical* hermeneutics attends to *how we read and study Scripture so as to hear God's address through it*.[14]

The most fundamental and important thing we can say about the Bible is that it is God's Word written, as Packer so ably defended. It came into existence over centuries as a deposit of God's journey with Israel (the Old Testament) and as a witness to the Christ event (the New Testament). This is the glory of its incarnate nature. It was written by humans at particular times and in particular places, and it bears all the marks of ancient Near Eastern culture (the Old Testament) and Greco-Roman culture (the New Testament). At the same time, Christians believe that God supervised the process of the Bible's production by his Spirit so that it is fully trustworthy (infallible) as God's Word to us.

The inspiration of the Bible is often expressed by saying that God is the primary author of Scripture. This means that ultimately the Bible is a unity and speaks with one voice, and thus any Christian biblical hermeneutic that fails to make the telos or goal of reading the Bible *to listen to God's address*

---

14. In chaps. 9–11, I develop three hermeneutical approaches that are central to this overarching biblical hermeneutic.

to us today falls short of taking Scripture seriously as God's Word. Because the Bible comes to us draped in ancient Near Eastern and Greco-Roman cultures, learning Hebrew and Greek is invaluable for serious study of the Bible since these are the main languages in which it was inspired. I encourage readers to study the original languages, while aware that for many this may not be possible.

Gadamer's hermeneutics gives us vital clues about how to read the Bible to hear God's address. In modern biblical interpretation, a common approach has said that if we just get the right method and apply it correctly, then we can be assured that we will get the right answers or the correct interpretation. Scholars disagree over what the right method is, but often they share the assumption that the right method yields the correct interpretation. Gadamer disagreed. He did not reject method, which is vitally important, but he resituated it.

Method Resituated

In Part I of his *Truth and Method*—note the title—Gadamer explores how we engage with an artwork. Think of one of your favorite pieces of art. How do you engage with it? Method would be one way. You could classify its type: painting, woodcut, screen print, sculpture, installation, landscape, portrait. You could examine the history of the artist and his or her times. You could investigate the medium: oak wood from South Africa, charcoal, pigments resourced from Iran. You could analyze the piece's style and composition. And so on. All such methods are valuable and will enhance your reception of the art, but it will be immediately apparent that you could engage in rigorous methodological analysis and miss encountering *the artwork itself*.

Hence, Gadamer resituates method within dialogue. One encounters art and is moved to engage with it. Gadamer refers to this engagement as a kind of dialogue. From one's preconceptions, a person asks questions of the artwork and sees how it "responds." Central to such dialogue is listening to and contemplating the art. Back and forth the dialogue goes until what Gadamer calls the fusion of horizons—the moment of understanding—takes place. Being attentive to one another is, in fact, how we dialogue with people. Art and texts are forms of human communication and merit the same sort of attentiveness and hospitality. Different methods, many of which we will explore in this book, find their place within the arc of dialogue.

If what Gadamer says is true of artworks and texts, how much more so is it true of the Bible as God's Word. The Bible comes to us as the deposit, like the silt from the river of God's journey with the ancient Near Eastern nation of Israel and through the Christ event. Israel and Jesus lived in the same world we do but centuries ago, and we will need to be attentive, to listen, to pose our questions in a back and forth movement until we begin to hear and understand so that we can receive the Bible as God's Word. Method is invaluable within that arc, but its attempt to be objective and scientific cannot replace the arc of dialogue.

Gadamer's approach also helps us open up the relationship between devotional and academic readings of the Bible. Devotional reading specializes in quiet, still listening and receptivity, just the sort of skills required for dialogue of any sort, including academic analysis of the Bible. Academic analysis should proceed from such listening and return to it, lest in our academic haste we simply impose our own views on the Bible.

The Bible on Fire

A sort of parable of this approach is Moses's encounter with the burning bush in Exodus 3. As a shepherd of his father-in-law's flocks, Moses would have been intimately familiar with the landscape around Sinai. But one day something different catches his attention: a bush burning but not consumed. His curiosity is piqued. He turns aside to the bush only to receive a much bigger surprise. God calls to him out of the middle of the bush: "Moses, Moses!" And so the dialogue begins. But this is no dialogue between equal parties. Moses is instructed to take his sandals off because he is standing on holy ground. God reveals himself to Moses as the God of his fathers, Abraham, Isaac, and Jacob (see Gen. 12–50), and then he draws Moses into his mission of liberating the Israelites from slavery. In the process, Moses is fully engaged; he asks his questions, and God responds.

The Bible is a burning bush. Through it we encounter the living God as he addresses us and invites us into relationship with himself, to become part of his people; he invites us to participate in the *missio Dei*, his great work in Christ, by his Spirit, of recovering his purposes for his creation and of leading it toward the destiny of a new heavens and a new earth, which he always intended for it. Mariano Magrassi expresses it this way: "The passage that leads to the understanding of Scripture leads to life in Christ. When the Scriptures are opened, he admits us to his private domain. Every deeper reading of the text is a movement toward him. The essential task of exegesis . . . is to apply everything to the mystery of Christ. . . . He is the one center where all the lines of the biblical universe meet."[15]

To hear God's address, our minds will indeed need to be fully engaged, but so, too, will our ears. As we receive and internalize God's Word, our hearts will be expanded so that we can run the way of his instruction into life.

Our Journey

On the following pages you will find an exercise in *lectio divina*. Such exercises occur after each chapter, intended to draw us back repeatedly into listening openly and receptively, even as—especially as—we dive into aspects of academic analysis of the Bible.

In the next chapter we will explore how to take hold of the Bible as a whole so that it takes hold of us as a whole. This is followed by a chapter discussing how we got the Bible, and chapters on a triadic approach to the Bible—the Bible as literature, history, and kerygma—and listening to and preaching the Bible. We conclude the book by tracing three major ways of receiving the Bible as God's Word: liturgically, ethically, and missionally.

DISCUSSION QUESTIONS

1. What might a famine of hearing God's Word look like today when we have so many Bibles?
2. Explain in your view what the Bible is.
3. What does your view of the Bible mean for how we should read it?
4. Consider reading through Psalm 119, making a list of all it teaches you about God's Word.
5. Explain the difference between a devotional and an academic reading of the Bible. Give examples.

15. Mariano Magrassi, *Praying the Bible: An Introduction to* Lectio Divina, trans. Edward Hagman (Collegeville, MN: Liturgical Press, 1998), 44.

6. How should the two kinds of reading relate to each other?

7. Reflect on when you have experienced God's Word most powerfully. What do you need to do to recover such a sense of his Word, if it has been lost?

8. What does it look like to run in the way of God's commands?

FURTHER READING

Magrassi, Mariano. *Praying the Bible: An Introduction to* Lectio Divina. Translated by Edward Hagman. Collegeville, MN: Liturgical Press, 1998. A friend introduced me to this book. It is extraordinary and by far the best I have come across on *lectio divina*.

Packer, J. I. *God Has Spoken: Revelation and the Bible.* 3rd ed. Grand Rapids: Baker, 1993.

Psalm 19. There are two major parts to the psalm, and scholars have often struggled to understand how the second part relates to the first. When you read the psalm, try to identify the two parts and how they relate.

Psalm 119. A psalm about God's instruction. When you read the psalm, consider what questions you bring to the psalm and what questions the psalm poses that you had not anticipated.

Wilken, Robert Louis. *The Spirit of Early Christian Thought: Seeking the Face of God.* New Haven: Yale University Press, 2003. See especially chapter 3, "The Face of God for Now." Wilken is always worth reading, and this book as a whole is a gift. Chapter 3 focuses particularly upon the reception of the Bible by the early church fathers.

DEVOTIONAL EXERCISE

Set aside at least twenty minutes for this exercise and those in the rest of the book.[16]

1. Slow down. Breathe in, breathe out. Connect with how you are: What are you feeling? What has been going on in your life? Remember you come to God *as you are.*

---

16. I am indebted to Sacred Space (https://www.sacredspace.ie/) for the shape of the devotional exercises in this book.

2. God is always waiting to greet us before we even arrive. Take a moment to greet God, and be thankful.

3. Be still and know that he is God.

   Amid our busy lives, stillness does not come easily.

   Choose a prayer word, such as "Father" or "Lord Jesus," to sink from your mind into your heart. Breathe in and breathe out, using your prayer word to quietly focus your attention on God.

   If this is difficult initially, keep it short (three to five minutes). With time you can expand it to ten minutes and beyond.

4. Read Psalm 119:32 slowly several times:

   I run in the path of your commands,
      for you have broadened my understanding [expanded my heart].

   Is there anything that catches your attention?
   Imagine yourself running like this.
   How does it feel?
   What do you see?
   How does the world look?
   Has your heart expanded?

5. Now imagine Jesus sitting comfortably in a chair opposite you. Say whatever you want to him, and listen to how he may respond to you.

6. If you have any requests of God, ask them now.

7. Spend another two minutes being still before God.

8. Carry Psalm 119:32 with you into your day, returning to it from time to time.

9. Conclude your time with this prayer:

   Glory be to the Father and to the Son and to the Holy Spirit. As it was in the beginning, is now, and ever shall be, world without end. Amen.

SUGGESTED ACTIVITIES ⎯⎯⎯⎯⎯⎯⎯⎯⎯⎯⎯⎯⎯⎯⎯⎯⎯⎯⎯⎯⎯⎯⎯

1. Either alone or with a group of friends, watch the film *Chariots of Fire*. Enjoy!

   How does the film relate to Psalm 119:32 and to your life?

2. Psalm 119 is by far the longest psalm. In the South African writer Herman Charles Bosman's *A Bekkersdal Marathon*, there is a hilarious story about the singing of the whole of Psalm 119 in a church service. You can read it here: https://caperebel.com/blogs/news/a-bekkersdal -marathon.

2

THE BIBLE AS A WHOLE

Consult your Bible's table of contents, and you will see that the (Protestant) Bible is made up of sixty-six books, thirty-nine in the Old Testament and twenty-seven in the New. These books were originally written in Hebrew and Aramaic (the Old Testament) and Greek (the New Testament). They came into existence over more than a thousand years, in cultures—ancient Near Eastern and Greco-Roman—very different from our own. As is often noted, the Bible is more like a library of books than a single book.

However, in many churches when the Bible is read, the reader ends by saying, "This is the Word of the Lord," and the congregation responds, "Thanks be to God." This simple exchange reminds us that Christians believe this collection of books is such a profound unity that no matter what part of it is read, we can proclaim that "this is the Word of the Lord." God is the primary author of Scripture, and he superintended what the Bible's secondary, human authors wrote, so that the Bible is a unity as God's Word written.

It may surprise you, then, that one of the great challenges in biblical studies today is how to understand the Bible as the unity it is. Modern study of the Bible has brought countless benefits, but too often it has so fragmented the Bible that readers stress its diversity and lose sight of its fundamental unity. If we are not careful, we end up with hundreds of jigsaw pieces that never fit together into a coherent picture, and the Bible becomes a never-ending puzzle.

There is, of course, real diversity in the Bible. There are two Testaments and many different types of literature, ranging from historical narrative to prophecy, law, poetry, Gospels, and letters. However, like the instruments in a glorious symphony, all these types of literature work together to create a great symphony revealing and recommending to us the God who has come to us in Jesus of Nazareth.

We begin, therefore, with the unity of the Bible. How do we take hold of the Bible as a whole so that it takes hold of us as a whole?

Enter "Biblical Theology"

"Biblical theology" may simply sound like theology that is biblical. This is incorrect. One way to understand biblical theology is to see it within the different disciplines that make up the field of theology. Theology is the academic discipline that deals with God and the world as revealed to us in Scripture. It has many subdisciplines. We can describe these as in the chart that follows:

Systematic Theology	The study of major doctrines, such as the doctrines of God, creation, the human person, the person and work of Christ, the Holy Spirit, the church, sin, and last things.
Biblical Studies	The study of the Bible (Old Testament and New Testament), including sections of the Bible, such as the Pentateuch (the first five books of the Old Testament) or the Gospels. Biblical theology is a subdiscipline of biblical studies, as described further below.
Church History	The study of the church and its development through the ages.
Practical Theology	The study of the practices of the church, such as preaching, leadership, counseling, and spiritual formation.
Missiology	The study of Christian mission, including its history and methodology.
Ethics	The study of how we should live today based on the teaching of God's Word.
World Religions	The study of the relationship between Christianity and other religions.
Philosophical Theology	The study of the relationship between philosophy and theology.

Biblical theology is part of the subdiscipline of biblical studies, but a very special part. Whereas systematic theology (or Christian doctrine) studies the major loci of Christian belief (e.g., the doctrines of God, creation, the church, etc.), biblical theology seeks to articulate the unity of the Bible *according to categories drawn from the Bible itself,* such as covenant and kingdom. If you think of the Bible as a house, then biblical theology is like studying the plumbing that traverses through the whole house. Or if you think of the Bible as a human body, then biblical theology is like studying the skeleton that holds the whole together.

My favorite image for the Bible is that of a grand cathedral. A cathedral has many entrances, some of which will only be known to the staff and not the public. By analogy, there are many legitimate ways to do biblical theology. William Dumbrell has, for example, written a number of books on Old Testament and biblical theology in which he takes a variety of approaches.

In his book *The End of the Beginning: Revelation 21–22 and the Old Testament,* Dumbrell identifies several major themes in Revelation 21–22 and then traces them through the whole Bible.[1] By comparison, in *The Faith of Israel* he goes through the Old Testament book by book.[2] And yet again, in his magisterial *Covenant and Creation,* he opens up the unity of the Old Testament inductively through an analysis of the major theme of covenant.[3] As you may have picked up, two of these are not actually *biblical* theologies but rather *Old Testament* theologies, since they do not cover the whole Bible. However, Dumbrell's three different approaches could all be applied to the whole Bible. My point is that there is not one way to do biblical theology. Just as with our cathedral, there are multiple entrances, and they all potentially give us fresh and informative perspectives on the Bible as a whole.

Where our image of a cathedral is also helpful is that while there are many entrances, there is only one main entrance. This allows us to ask the question, Is there a main entrance to the Bible that best enables us to see the whole? In my view there is, and we find it in Jesus's teaching. The Gospels are clear that the main theme of Jesus's teaching was the kingdom of God.

---

1. William J. Dumbrell, *The End of the Beginning: Revelation 21–22 and the Old Testament* (Sydney: Lancer, 1986).

2. William J. Dumbrell, *The Faith of Israel: A Theological Survey of the Old Testament,* 2nd ed. (Grand Rapids: Baker Academic, 2002).

3. William J. Dumbrell, *Covenant and Creation: An Old Testament Covenant Theology,* rev. ed. (Milton Keynes, UK: Paternoster, 2013).

Mark 1:14–15, for example, provides a pithy summary of what Jesus taught as he went around preaching and teaching: "After John was put in prison, Jesus went into Galilee, proclaiming the good news of God. 'The time has come,' he said. '*The kingdom of God* has come near. Repent and believe the good news!'" (emphasis added).

These short two verses are pregnant with significance. The Gospel of Matthew uses "the kingdom of heaven" as a synonym for "the kingdom of God," choosing a Jewish way of referring to God by God's place—that is, "heaven"—rather than using the name "God." John has his own vocabulary for the kingdom of God in his Gospel.

What is the kingdom of God? Alas, the Gospel writers do not provide a handy definition. However, there are many clues in Jesus's teaching and in his deeds as recorded in the Gospels. Already in the verses above, "the good news" provides us with a major clue. The word translated as good news is *euangelion* in the Greek. It has its background in Isaiah and other parts of the Old Testament. *Euangelion* is not just good news that, for example, the weekend is coming after a hard week. It is epochal news, news that the turning point in history has arrived. God is intervening such that things will never be the same again. And this intervention has everything to do with God's reign, so that N. T. Wright defines the kingdom of God simply as the reign of Israel's god. The kingdom of God is all about God's intervention in history through Jesus to recover his purposes for his creation and to lead the whole creation toward the destiny that he always intended for it. "Kingdom" is thus about both God's reign and the realm over which he reigns: the whole creation. A metaphor for becoming a Christian in Mark's Gospel is entering the kingdom. We need to do this individually, but once we enter we become part of God's kingdom purposes, actively living under his reign as he works by his Spirit to lead us and the whole creation toward the second coming of Jesus, when he will usher in the new heavens and the new earth.

Closely related to the kingdom of God in the New Testament is the theme of covenant in the Old. God administers his reign or rule over his people in the Old Testament through a series of covenants, most notably the covenants with Noah and Abraham, the Sinai covenant, the Davidic covenant, and the new covenant prophesied by Jeremiah. In my opinion, Dumbrell is correct that the basic covenantal text in the Old Testament is Genesis 1–2, to which all the other covenants look back and are themselves about God's work in history through his people Israel to recover his purpose for his whole creation.[4] At the Passover meal that Jesus shared with his disciples shortly before his betrayal, crucifixion, and resurrection, he spoke of "the blood of the new covenant," using the Passover rituals to symbolize his forthcoming death as the Lamb who takes away the sin of the world. This alerts us to the fact that a major way in which the Old Testament relates to the New Testament is that Jesus fulfills the Old Testament.

Indeed, one simply cannot understand the New Testament without the Old. You can begin with Jesus proclaiming the kingdom of God, but this will soon push you into asking questions like the following:

- Hasn't God always been King?
- What went wrong to cause so many people to rebel against his rule?
- How do the Old Testament and Israel fit into the coming of the kingdom with Jesus?

In other words, the minute we attend closely to the major themes of covenant and kingdom—great doorways at the entrance to the cathedral of the Bible—we are compelled to trace out and narrate the grand story the Bible tells from Genesis through Revelation. My proposal is thus that the best way to take hold of the Bible as a whole, so that it takes hold of us as a whole, is to read it as a grand, sprawling, capacious metanarrative[5] that tells the true story of the whole world.

Lesslie Newbigin: Indwelling the Story of the Bible

Lesslie Newbigin, the great missionary and missiologist of the twentieth century, became a Christian at Cambridge University. He and his wife later went to India as missionaries, where Lesslie spent the major years of his career exploring how the gospel encountered Indian culture. He tells the fascinating story of a meeting with the Hindu scholar Chaturvedi Badrinath, who said to him:

> I can't understand why you missionaries present the Bible to us in India as a book of religion. It is not a book of religion—and anyway we have

---

4. Dumbrell, *Covenant and Creation*, chap. 1.
5. I am leaning here on Eugene Peterson, "Living into God's Story," https://missionworld view.com/wp-content/uploads/2020/06/ea8a85_f728f22e39d8426e9e35f0ce85e0f4e2.pdf.

plenty of books of religion in India. We don't need any more! I find in your
Bible a unique interpretation of universal history, the history of the whole
of creation and the history of the human race. And therefore a unique
interpretation of the human person as a responsible actor in history.
That is unique. There is nothing else in the whole religious literature of
the world to put alongside it.[6]

When he retired, Lesslie and his wife returned to England, where he—
from my perspective—began some of his most fruitful years of ministry.
Among so many other things, he helped the church see the modern world
as *the* great missional challenge, and he encouraged seeing the Bible as
the book that tells the true story of the world and invites us to indwell that
story as our default mode of existence.

"Story" does not mean unhistorical. In recent years literary scholars and
philosophers have shown that both historiography and fiction make use of
the same narrative tools to tell their "stories." When we speak of the Bible
as a story we are not referring to the Bible as fiction—although fiction can
certainly be true in its own way. Rather, we are arguing that the overarching shape of the Bible is that of a narrative: it has a beginning, something
major going wrong, an unfolding plot to rectify what has gone wrong, and
a conclusion. What I am arguing, with Newbigin, is that the overarching
story the Bible tells is the *true* story of the whole world.

It should not surprise us that the Bible has a story shape to it. In and through
the Bible, God introduces himself to us and invites us to become part of what
he is doing in his creation. Reflect for a moment on how people get to know
one another. You meet someone, you arrange to have coffee together, and
sooner or later you will find yourself saying to the other person, "Tell me your
story. Tell me about yourself." The way we reveal ourselves to other people
is through our stories. And the way God reveals himself to us is through the
record of his journey with his Old Testament people, Israel, which climaxes in
his revelation of himself in his Son, Jesus. Newbigin thus summarizes the story
of the Bible as the move from a garden (Eden) to a city (the new Jerusalem).

In recent decades scholars have also come to realize that not only do
individuals understand and reveal themselves through their stories, but our
view of the world, our worldviews, are grounded in stories we tell about the

6. Lesslie Newbigin, *A Walk through the Bible* (London: Triangle, 1999), 4. See also
Lesslie Newbigin, *The Gospel in a Pluralist Society* (Grand Rapids: Eerdmans, 1989), 89.

world—whether it be the big bang story of evolution or the creation-fall-redemption story of the Bible. The good news about this is that once we read the Bible as the true story of the world, not only will the Bible show us who we are, but it will also provide us with the lenses through which to see the world aright. Calvin comparably likens the Bible to a pair of glasses that bring the world into focus and help us see it as God's creation.

It is worth pausing to consider Newbigin's exhortation for us to "indwell" the biblical story. *Dwell* is an interesting word. You may recall the controversial decision several years ago by a slim majority of UK citizens to leave the European Union in what became known as Brexit. One analysis of Brexit distinguished between "Somewheres" and "Nowheres." Nowheres are people who feel they could live in any major city. They are not deeply rooted in one place; instead, they believe they could happily live in most major cities as long as the normal conveniences were close at hand. Somewheres are different. They are connected to specific places and feel this connection strongly. They do not think that they could as happily live elsewhere. The analysis suggested that Nowheres were more likely to remain in the EU, whereas Somewheres were more likely to vote to leave the EU because they felt that it was changing their country beyond recognition.

Whatever we think about Brexit, when it comes to the Bible we are called to be Somewheres. We are to indwell the biblical story so intimately, to become so familiar with its geography, that it becomes our story, our default mode when things go wrong. We are to think out of it, live out of it, and grow ever more deeply into it.

Now, of course, we will only be able to do that if we know the biblical story well. A person can be doing very advanced studies as a Christian scholar in some discipline and still be unable to tell the biblical story. In my opinion, we need to be able to tell the main contours of the biblical story in about twenty minutes. How might we go about doing this?

Tom Wright: The Bible as a Drama in Five Acts

In 1991 Tom Wright (aka N. T. Wright) published an important article entitled "How Can the Bible Be Authoritative?"[7] Wright points out that in

---

7. N. T. Wright, "How Can the Bible Be Authoritative?," *Vox Evangelica* 21 (1991): 7–32, https://ntwrightpage.com/2016/07/12/how-can-the-bible-be-authoritative/. Quotations throughout this section are from this article with page numbers noted in parentheses.

the Bible it is God who is the ultimate authority and in whom authority is vested. He encourages us to look to the Bible to see how God exercises his authority, and he argues that "God's authority vested in scripture is designed, as all God's authority is designed, to liberate human beings, to judge and condemn evil and sin in the world in order to set people free to be fully human. That's what God is in the business of doing" (16). He shows how this is the case throughout the Old Testament and then argues that as a result of the Christ event, "in order that the church may be the church—may be the people of God for the world—God, by that same Holy Spirit, equips men in the first generation to write the new covenant documentation. This is to be the new covenant documentation which gives the foundation charter and the characteristic direction and identity to the people of God, who are to be the people of God for the world" (17).

Wright poses the vital question, How might God use the Bible to exercise his authority? He proposes that we imagine a play by the great playwright William Shakespeare is found, but the fifth act in the play has been lost.[8] The initial four acts are so rich and creative, brimming with fascinating characters and plot development, that it is widely agreed that the play simply must be performed and staged. One way forward would be to commission a contemporary playwright to write the final act, but this is resisted. Far better, it is argued, for experienced, professional Shakespearean actors to be identified and to be asked to immerse themselves in the initial four acts and then to develop the fifth act themselves. Such development would involve both consistency with the first four acts and innovation (18–19).

Wright proposes that this provides a good model for how we might think of the authority of the Bible. There are four initial acts (19):

- Creation
- Fall
- Israel
- Jesus

8. Wright moves easily between the categories of story and drama, but they are not exactly the same thing. See my discussion in Craig G. Bartholomew, *Introducing Biblical Hermeneutics: A Comprehensive Framework for Hearing God in Scripture* (Grand Rapids: Baker Academic, 2015).

The New Testament is the first scene in the final, fifth act, also provid-
ing clues as to how the play ends. "The church would then live under the
'authority' of the extant story, being required to offer something between
an improvisation and an actual performance of the final act" (19). Wright
describes the New Testament as the "charter" for the church, living as it
does between the coming of the kingdom in Jesus and its final consummation at the end of the ages. The first three acts are vital for understanding
acts 4 and 5, but in Wright's evocative words, it is inappropriate for them
to be picked up and hurled into act 5 without careful consideration. Wright
is clear that "the Old Testament has the authority that an earlier act of the
play would have, no more, no less" (19). It is not the charter for the church
in the same way as the New Testament. Out of this Wright develops what
we might call a *missional* understanding of the authority of the Bible:

> God wants the church to lift up its eyes and see the field ripe for harvest,
> and to go out, armed with the authority of scripture; not just to get its own
> life right within a Christian ghetto, but to use the authority of scripture
> to declare to the world authoritatively that Jesus is Lord. And, since the
> New Testament is the covenant charter of the people of God, the Holy
> Spirit, I believe, desires and longs to do this task in each generation by
> reawakening people to the freshness of that covenant, and hence sum-
> moning them to fresh covenant tasks. The phrase "authority of scripture,"
> therefore, is a sort of shorthand for the fact that the creator and covenant
> God uses this book as his means of equipping and calling the church for
> these tasks. (21–22)

Wright's proposal is rich and creative. I would nuance his articulation
of God's authority slightly, noting that God exercises his authority as Creator and Redeemer. The doctrine of providence flows from the doctrine of
creation and shows us that God sustains the world in existence and accompanies and guides it to its destination, as well as rules over it. Redemption
or salvation fits within this context—as Ola Tjørhom says, creation is the
very stuff of redemption[9]—as God's great mission to retrieve his purposes
for his creation, to eradicate sin and evil, and to lead creation to the goal
he always intended for it, so that the whole redounds to his glory.

9. Ola Tjørhom, *Embodied Faith: Reflections on a Materialist Spirituality* (Grand Rapids:
Eerdmans, 2009), 36.

One could say that Wright has taken Newbigin's idea of indwelling the biblical story and provided a sophisticated model for what that might look like. His model helps us see where we fit in the biblical story. It also highlights our responsibility to be shaped by the story and to use its insights for living the story today and telling it as the good news it is in both word and deed. Lest we should think this obvious, the New Zealand sociologist John Carroll argues that it is the one thing the church has signally failed to do. In his *The Existential Jesus*, Carroll argues that "the waning of Christianity in the West is easy to explain. The Christian churches have comprehensively failed to retell their foundation story in a way that might speak to the times."[10] We should not, therefore, underestimate just how significant it might be for us to recover the Bible as the true story of the whole world. How exactly might we retell the biblical story today?

The Bible as a Drama in Six Acts

Mike Goheen and I recognized the need not just to talk about the Bible as a grand narrative but to do the hard work of actually telling the biblical story. In our *The Drama of Scripture: Finding Our Place in the Biblical Story*, we draw on both Newbigin and Wright, as well as other sources. However, rather than five acts in the drama of the Bible, we identified the following six:

- Act 1   God Establishes His Kingdom: Creation
- Act 2   Rebellion in the Kingdom: Fall
- Act 3   The King Chooses Israel: Salvation Initiated
- Act 4   The Coming of the King: Salvation Accomplished
- **Act 5   Spreading the News of the King: The Mission of the Church**
- Act 6   The Return of the King: Redemption Completed

We noted above that the kingdom of God is the main theme of Jesus's teaching, and you can see in our outline how God's kingship shapes the whole drama. Act 5 is in bold because this is the act in which we find ourselves and are invited consciously to inhabit. Herberg evokes this invitation exquisitely: "It is (to borrow from Kierkegaard) as though we sat witness-

10. John Carroll, *The Existential Jesus* (Washington, DC: Counterpoint, 2007), 7.

ing some tremendous epic drama being performed on a vast stage, when suddenly the chief character of the drama, who is also its director, steps forward to the front of the stage, fixes his eye upon us, points his finger at us, and calls out: 'You, you're wanted. Come up here. Take your part!'"[11]

The main character and director is, of course, the living God. If we are to take our part in God's great mission, then we need to know the biblical story inside out, so that we can play our part with excellence and enhance the reputation of the main character and director. There are good resources available in this respect; for now we will outline the biblical story so that as we progress through this book we are conscious of its main contours.

The Bible begins with these epochal words: "In the beginning God created the heavens and the earth." "The heavens and the earth" is a merism that, by referring to the two extremities of the creation, speaks of all creation. As John says of the Word, "Apart from him nothing came into existence that has come into existence" (John 1:3 AT). Every single aspect of the entire creation owes its origin to God. In many dramas the setting can change, but once we see how comprehensive creation is, we realize that this first act is the setting for the entire drama of the Bible.

And what a setting it is. Through days 1–6 of Genesis 1:1–2:3, God differentiates his creation into the three major places of earth, sea, and sky, and then he populates each of those areas. The first high point is reached with the creation of humankind in Genesis 1:26–28, male and female in God's image. Remarkably, humans, who are so different from God, are made *like him* as relational creatures called to steward his creation and develop its hidden potentials so that more and more it resounds to his glory. The second high point is reached on day 7. God has completed his work of creation; he contemplates it and declares it "very good!"

The whole world is made as the best of homes for humans, but they can only live in particular places. So in Genesis 2 God establishes the first couple in a large park called Eden, which means "delight." Everything they need to flourish is there. They are called to maintain and develop the park so that everything, including the animals, flourishes. God would come and walk and talk with them, a sign of the intimate relationship with God for which humans are designed.

11. Will Herberg, *Faith Enacted as History: Essays in Biblical Theology*, ed. Bernhard W. Anderson (Philadelphia: Westminster, 1976), 41.

The only thing the first couple is not to do is to eat from the tree of the knowledge of good and evil. This is a strange name for a tree and indicates that the tree is symbolic of humans choosing not to live under God's reign but to become a law unto themselves, what we call human autonomy. Tragically and catastrophically, the first couple is tempted by the serpent, and they succumb to the temptation. Immediately, they start to feel shame and hide from God. This is act 2: the fall into sin.

The first couple is cast out of Eden, the way back barred to them. Judgment is pronounced on them and the serpent. Once their relationship with God is broken by sin, sin and its effects start to seep into all areas of life. The first couple's sons, Cain and Abel, grow into manhood, but horrifically, Cain murders Abel out of jealous anger. As the human race develops, the distortion of sin manifests itself in myriad ways, until God says enough; he decides to start again with Noah and his descendants after the judgment of a great flood on the earth. But soon sin is dominant again and climaxes in the people of the earth coming together to build a huge tower at Babel, reaching up into the heavens, a symbol of a false unity resting on human pride and autonomy. To prevent their attempt at another such project, God disperses the nations and also ensures that they will struggle to communicate with one another.

At this point in the story, it seems as though God's kingdom project has run into the ground. What will he do? God does not give up on his project; indeed, already in Genesis 3:15, when he pronounced judgment on the first couple and the serpent, God promised that a descendant of the first couple would arise who would crush the head of the serpent and incur serious wounding in the process. What God does is to call one man, Abraham, the father of the nation Israel. This brings us into act 3: the King chooses Israel and initiates salvation.

God enters into a covenant relationship with Abraham, promising him numerous descendants, a relationship with God, and a land for his descendants. From Genesis 12 to the end of Joshua is the story of the gradual fulfillment of each of these promises. Abraham's grandson Jacob ends up in Egypt with his sons, and there they expand numerically over a period of some four hundred years. When a new pharaoh comes to power in Egypt and identifies the multiplying Israelites—the promise that Abraham's descendants would be numerous has been fulfilled—as *the* national threat, he makes their life as difficult as possible, even adopting a policy of euthanasia for all Israelite baby boys. Ironically, one of these boys, Moses, is rescued by

Pharaoh's daughter and is raised and educated in Pharaoh's own household. God calls Moses to liberate the Israelites from their servitude, and a major showdown emerges between Moses (and the Lord) and Pharaoh. The Lord casts plague after horrible plague on Egypt, but Pharaoh refuses to let the Israelites go. Finally, in the last plague the angel of death visits Egypt, and all their firstborn die. The angel spares the Israelites because of lamb's blood painted on the doors of their houses; he passes over their houses, an event remembered in the great Feast of Passover. Finally, Pharaoh relents and orders the Israelites out of Egypt.

Moses leads the liberated slaves out of Egypt, but soon Pharaoh changes his mind and sends his army after them—only to be crushed in the Red Sea. The Lord, not Pharaoh, is shown to be God. Moses leads the Israelites to Mount Sinai, where God descends on the mountain in fire and lightning. The people get to meet the Lord and through the mediation of Moses are established by covenant as his people, with laws given by God to regulate their lives as such. Once the covenant has been formalized, the Lord provides instructions for the building of his residence in the midst of the Israelites. The Israelites build the portable, royal residence, known as the tabernacle, and when it is consecrated, God's presence fills it. God's promise to Abraham about a special relationship with his descendants is fulfilled in a remarkable fashion.

The remaining promise to Abraham is that of the land. The Israelites' repeated grumbling and refusal to trust the Lord delay their conquest of the promised land, but after a generation has died out, the people enter and conquer the land under Joshua's leadership. All three of the major promises to Abraham are fulfilled: numerous descendants, a special relationship, and a land of their own, Canaan, with the living God in their midst.

Israel is poised for greatness. It seems they are set to fulfill God's vocation for them—namely, to be a window through which the nations could peer to see what truly human life looks like.

Instead, the story from this point on goes steadily downhill, with a few high points. In the book of Judges, after the death of Joshua, the people begin a cyclical pattern: they descend into anarchy; God hands individual tribes over to foreign powers; the people cry out to the Lord for help; he raises up military figures, called judges, to rescue them; repeat. But this circular process becomes a downward spiral, as the judges themselves look more and more like the rebellious Israelites.

The Israelites realize something is wrong and come up with a solution: they need a king like the other nations. God allows them to appoint a king, Saul, but warns of the dangers of kingship. The second king, David, is far better than the first, but he himself commits adultery and then murder as he tries to hide his sin. David's son Solomon succeeds him, and under him the temple is built and consecrated in Jerusalem; God now has a fixed abode in the midst of Israel. Solomon is gifted with wisdom but still behaves foolishly at times, and after his death, Israel splits into a northern and a southern kingdom.

Israel occupies a small land at the intersection of the great empires of the day. Its very existence depends on God's favor. Alas, the Northern Kingdom persists in its rebellion against God and is exiled by the Assyrians in 722 BC. Despite God repeatedly sending prophets to call his people back to himself and his ways, the Southern Kingdom follows suit in 587 BC, when the Babylonians sack the temple and take the people into exile.

Once again God's kingdom project seems to have run aground. However, through his prophets God continues to speak to his people, assuring them they will return to the land and promising them that his words will still come to fulfillment through a figure called the Messiah. After some seventy years, many of the Israelites from the Southern Kingdom return to Judah, where they rebuild the temple and the city walls. However, foreign powers continue to threaten God's people: the Persians, the Greeks, and then the Romans, and the Israelites chafe under foreign rule.

From the end of the Old Testament until the start of the New, there is a period of some four hundred years during which the voice of prophecy goes silent. This is not to say God is not quietly at work. He is! The Old Testament is translated into Greek, synagogues are established across the Roman Empire, and the Romans establish the Pax Romana, peace across a vast stretch of territory with good roads constructed to facilitate travel far and wide. Among the Jews several groups develop: the Pharisees, the Sadducees, the Zealots, and the Essenes. These groups have different ideas about how to respond to Roman domination. The Zealots, for example, are all for getting an army together to overthrow the Romans. The Essenes, by comparison, withdraw into a kind of monastic quietude. However, all of them look toward the day when God will intervene and usher in his kingdom, even if they have very different ideas of how that might happen and what it will involve.

And then one day the voice of prophecy returns. News gets around that an unusually dressed man who eats locusts and honey is preaching in the wilderness, telling the Jews that the King is on his way and they need to prepare for his coming by repenting and being baptized. And so begins act 4, the center of the biblical story. This unusual man is John the Baptist, and he is preparing the way for the arrival of Jesus.

Born of the virgin Mary, Jesus remains in relative obscurity for the first thirty years of his life, until John the Baptist begins announcing his arrival. Through his baptism by John and his searing temptations in the wilderness, Jesus solidifies his vocation as Savior of the world with crystal clarity. He calls twelve disciples to accompany him on his public ministry; just as there were twelve tribes in Israel, these twelve disciples are intended to be the foundation of the new people of God. Jesus moves around teaching, preaching, healing, and doing other miracles. The main theme of his teaching is the kingdom of God, but what shocks his hearers is his declaration that the kingdom has come with his arrival! Through his teaching and miracles, he also claims to be God, a terrible offense to the monotheistic Jewish leaders.

Jesus's public ministry lasts about three years, and there is so much to tell about this extraordinary time. As he touches lives in profound ways, heals many who are considered incurable, draws followers from the margins and the centers of life, it becomes impossible for the Jewish leaders to ignore him. Opposition grows and comes to a climax at the Passover festival in Jerusalem during the third year of his public ministry. Jesus openly proclaims himself to be the promised Messiah, and the opposition to him erupts. Betrayed to the Jewish leaders by one of his twelve disciples, Judas, Jesus is handed over to the Romans for trial and eventually condemned to the most awful death by crucifixion.

Yet again, it seems as though God's kingdom purposes might have run aground. Certainly that is what his disciples and many of his followers must have thought. But early on the third day, when some of his followers go to Jesus's tomb, it is empty. Jesus has risen from the dead! Over the next forty days, he shows himself repeatedly to his disciples and followers, demonstrating that he has conquered death and is alive. On the fortieth day, he arranges to meet his disciples in Galilee, charges them with the mission of spreading the news about him throughout the world, and then ascends into heaven.

What now? Fast-forward ten days to the Feast of Pentecost when Jesus's followers are gathered together in Jerusalem. Suddenly, there is the noise of a great wind, and tongues of fire settle on the head of each follower, and they speak in the many different languages of those gathered in Jerusalem for Pentecost, telling the news of Jesus in people's individual languages. The promised outpouring of the Holy Spirit has begun, inaugurating act 5: the mission of the church.

That day Jesus's disciple Peter preaches an extraordinary sermon explaining to the crowd what is happening and telling them the good news about Jesus. Some three thousand people are converted. The book of Acts tells the exhilarating story of how the news about Jesus spreads from Jerusalem to Judea and ultimately to the ends of the earth, attracting converts— and opposition—wherever it goes. One of the greatest opponents of Christianity is converted: Paul, who goes on to become the great missionary to the gentiles, establishing churches in major cities across the Roman Empire. Twelve of his letters, through which he demonstrates pastoral care to various churches and church leaders, are in the New Testament.

From the inception of the church, one major characteristic of the early Christians is that they devote themselves to the teaching of the apostles, a name for the initial group of disciples. Why? Because the apostles were eyewitnesses of Jesus's public ministry, and it is in and through their testimony that the early Christians encounter Jesus. It is this apostolic testimony that is eventually written down to become the four Gospels and the rest of the New Testament.

Over centuries the church spreads around the world and eventually comes to our towns, our cities, our villages. It is now over two thousand years since the outpouring of the Spirit on Pentecost, but the work of mission continues. It has reached us, and we are called to live out the good news of Jesus in every part of our lives and to tell that news to the world. We live in act 5, the age of mission, in which all are invited to enter the kingdom of God and in which God's people are called to live under God's reign as a sign of that kingdom.

Jesus's first coming was not at all what most people expected. For those with eyes to see, it was apparent that he was indeed the Son of God, but he was incognito, divested of the glory and sovereignty rightly his. The next act, act 6, will occur when Jesus returns in triumph and glory, no longer incognito, but now apparent to all as the living, conquering King come to judge the living and the dead and to usher in the new heavens and the new earth, a renewed creation cleansed of all evil.

That End Which Is No End

Act 6 will usher us into an end which is no end but a whole new beginning. We have been through the story of the Bible from a thousand feet, as it were, noting the great landmarks. My hope is that this provides us with a sense of how the Bible fits together, of what a remarkable story it is, and how we need to know it in far greater detail if we are genuinely to indwell it. That should be the goal of your further work in biblical studies. However, already we can see that the Bible provides us with a framework for understanding the world and ourselves, and even as we continue on our journey, let us not forget that in our studies—not least our biblical studies—we are called to think and live out of this true story of the world.

DISCUSSION QUESTIONS

1. What is biblical theology? Make sure you understand this. I recommend going back to the definition in the chapter and learning it by heart.
2. How is biblical theology different from systematic theology? Explain.
3. There are different approaches to biblical theology. Which approach do I recommend in this chapter?
4. See if you can remember the six acts in the drama of Scripture. Again, I recommend going back to them in this chapter and memorizing them.
5. Which act are we presently in?
6. Lesslie Newbigin encourages us to indwell the biblical story. Have a go at this by thinking through one of the following topics from the story: marriage, government, or worship.

FURTHER READING

Bartholomew, Craig G., and Michael W. Goheen. *The Drama of Scripture: Finding Our Place in the Biblical Story*. 2nd ed. Grand Rapids: Baker Academic, 2014.

Bartholomew, Craig G., and Paige P. Vanosky. *The 30-Minute Bible: God's Story for Everyone*. Downers Grove, IL: InterVarsity, 2021.

Newbigin, Lesslie. *A Walk through the Bible*. London: Triangle, 1999.

Wright, N. T. "How Can the Bible Be Authoritative?" *Vox Evangelica* 21 (1991): 7–32. https://ntwrightpage.com/2016/07/12/how-can-the-bible-be-authoritative/.

DEVOTIONAL EXERCISE

1. Come to stillness before God, quietly and attentively. For five minutes or so, be still and know that he is God.

2. Be honest with God about how you are doing.

3. Read through the story of the walk to Emmaus slowly several times. Imagine yourself as one of the two disciples. What do you feel, see, and hear?

   Luke 24:13–35

   Now that same day two of them were going to a village called Emmaus, about seven miles from Jerusalem. They were talking with each other about everything that had happened. As they talked and discussed these things with each other, Jesus himself came up and walked along with them; but they were kept from recognizing him.

   He asked them, "What are you discussing together as you walk along?"

   They stood still, their faces downcast. One of them, named Cleopas, asked him, "Are you the only one visiting Jerusalem who does not know the things that have happened there in these days?"

   "What things?" he asked.

   "About Jesus of Nazareth," they replied. "He was a prophet, powerful in word and deed before God and all the people. The chief priests and our rulers handed him over to be sentenced to death, and they crucified him; but we had hoped that he was the one who was going to redeem Israel. And what is more, it is the third day since all this took place. In addition, some of our women amazed us. They went to the tomb early this morning but didn't find his body. They came and told us that they had seen a vision of angels, who said he was alive. Then some of our companions went to the tomb and found it just as the women had said, but they did not see Jesus."

He said to them, "How foolish you are, and how slow to believe all that the prophets have spoken! Did not the Messiah have to suffer these things and then enter his glory?" And beginning with Moses and all the Prophets, he explained to them what was said in all the Scriptures concerning himself.

As they approached the village to which they were going, Jesus continued on as if he were going farther. But they urged him strongly, "Stay with us, for it is nearly evening; the day is almost over." So he went in to stay with them.

When he was at the table with them, he took bread, gave thanks, broke it and began to give it to them. Then their eyes were opened and they recognized him, and he disappeared from their sight. They asked each other, "Were not our hearts burning within us while he talked with us on the road and opened the Scriptures to us?"

They got up and returned at once to Jerusalem. There they found the Eleven and those with them, assembled together and saying, "It is true! The Lord has risen and has appeared to Simon." Then the two told what had happened on the way, and how Jesus was recognized by them when he broke the bread.

Have you ever experienced a "burning heart" when reading the Bible? If so, return in your memory to such occasions.

How do you experience the Bible today?

What would it be like if Jesus opened the Scriptures to you today?

4. Imagine Jesus sitting next to you. Talk to him about how you experience the Bible. Ask him to open the Bible to you.

5. Conclude your time with this prayer:

Lord Jesus, help us so to attend to your Word that again and again our hearts may burn as we discover you in and through the Bible. Amen.

SUGGESTED ACTIVITIES ───────────────────────────────────┐

1. Browse biblical and Old Testament and New Testament theologies in your library or online. See if you can identify some of the different approaches they take. Make a list.

2. With a few of your friends, attempt to tell the story of the Bible using the six acts in this chapter. How well are you able to do this?

3

HOW WE GOT THE BIBLE

In many books, a chapter with the title "How We Got the Bible" would deal with the formation of the canon—namely, the list and nature of authoritative books in the Bible. It is common to find such discussion centered around the *terminus ad quem* of canon formation: the time by which books or sections of books—such as the Pentateuch or Gospels—were accepted as canonical. There is clearly value in such investigations, but such an approach is in danger of putting the cart before the horse. Just as N. T. Wright insists on locating the authority of the Bible in God, so, too, the emergence of the Bible should be grounded in God's revelation of himself.

Taking into account the nature of God and of ourselves as creatures, the logic of revelation is impeccable. The United Kingdom, where I live, is a monarchy at the head of which is His Majesty the King, Charles III. Now imagine if I decided that I wanted to get to know the king *personally*. I did not want to read a book about him, of which there are many, but I wanted to get to know *him*. I could write to Buckingham Palace, I could go there requesting to see him, but none of this would enable me to get to meet him, let alone to know him personally. He is the king, and thus any initiative would have to come from him. Only at his invitation would I be able to visit, and only if he chose to disclose his life to me—something he is wisely very cautious of doing—would I be able to get to know him.

If this is true of the king, how much more is it true of the living God who dwells, as the New Testament says, in unapproachable light. It is only when God takes the initiative, makes contact with us, tells us about himself, and shows himself to us that we have any hope of getting to know him personally. This was true even of the first couple in Eden. It was only as God walked and talked with them that they would have gotten to know God personally. Again, the *how much more* argument follows. As fallen human beings, sinful and rebellious, how much more does our getting to know God depend upon him graciously taking the initiative to introduce himself to us, to forgive our sins and rebellion, and to restore us to a deep personal relationship with himself.

The good news is that this is precisely what God loves to do. In many ways the Bible is the record of him doing so throughout history, and it is such self-disclosure by God that underlies the Bible and led to its formation.

The God Who Reveals Himself

We do not know what Adam and Eve talked with God about in Eden, but doubtless they grew in their knowledge of him through such meetings. After the fall, God's relationship with humans becomes far more complex because of our sin and rebellion, but in his grace he never stops initiating relationships with his image bearers. The Bible is filled with God's initiative, from his seeking out Adam and Eve when they are hiding from him (Gen. 3), to his appeal to Cain (Gen. 4), to his call of Abraham (Gen. 12), to his friendship with Moses and the prophets, to his revelation of himself to Israel (Exod. 19–24), all culminating in his becoming incarnate in Jesus of Nazareth. As John 1:18 puts it, "No one has ever seen God, but the one and only Son, who is himself God and is in closest relationship with the Father, has made him known."

God's encounter with Moses at the burning bush is a good example of the personal nature of God's disclosure of himself. Moses is rescued from death by the compassion of Pharaoh's daughter—Kass speaks delightfully of a conspiracy of compassion—and is raised in Pharaoh's court.[1] By this time the Israelites have been in Egypt for four hundred years, and perhaps Abraham, Isaac, and Jacob are distant memories, if even that. From Exodus 2:11 we learn

---

1. Leon R. Kass, *Founding God's Nation: Reading Exodus* (New Haven: Yale University Press, 2021), 42–43.

that Moses has a sense that the Israelites are "his people," but we have no idea how much he knows about God's journey with the patriarchs and his promises to them. Moses needs to personally get to know God and be formed as a leader if he is to play his role in the drama of the exodus about to take place.

After fleeing from Egypt, Moses lives with the Midianites and works as a shepherd, a far cry from the ostentation and sophistication of Pharaoh's royal court. However, it is in the wilderness near Mount Sinai that God chooses to meet with Moses. The wilderness lacks the distractions of urban life, and as a shepherd Moses would have been very familiar with and attentive to the landscape. He would have known where good pasture was to be found for his flock and would have been on the lookout for good grazing, attentive to the possibility of predators. It is this very attentiveness that God uses to introduce himself to Moses. God catches Moses's attention through something very familiar to him—a bush—and something very unfamiliar—a bush that burns with fire and yet is not consumed. This is the extraordinary condescension of God; he approaches in terms that Moses can understand and yet that vastly exceed those very terms.

God takes the initiative in manifesting himself in this sensory way in a bush, then—when Moses turns toward the bush—by calling out to him by name: "Moses, Moses." God both acts and speaks, and both elements are central to his self-revelation to Moses. We need to feel the profoundly personal nature of this encounter with God. God knows Moses and calls him by name. Because God is God, the encounter is not one between equals— Moses has to take off his sandals because he is on holy ground—but it is truly interpersonal. God introduces himself to Moses, tells him what he is up to, sets out the role Moses is to play in God's work of rescuing the Israelites, and a dialogue ensues. Certainly, Moses learns *about* God in this encounter—Exodus 3 is filled with language of divine action—but in such a disclosure event, God not only offers knowledge about himself but offers himself. John 17:3 tells us that eternal life is to know God. This certainly includes knowing about God, but as with Moses it is far more. Knowledge of God is always deeply and wonderfully personal.

God's revelation of himself to Moses near Mount Sinai leads to his self-disclosure to the Israelites as a whole and his entering into a covenant relationship with them as a people (Exod. 19–24). Yet again it is himself that God offers. In Exodus 19:4 God compares the exodus from Egypt to him flying the Israelites out of Egypt like an eagle with her young on her back; the destination of their deliverance is God himself: "and [I] brought you to myself." Following the ratification of the covenant in Exodus 24, at God's command the Israelites build the tabernacle, God's portable, royal residence that will accompany them as they journey to the promised land. Eventually, under King Solomon God's permanent palace, the temple, will be built as God's fixed abode amid his people in the land.

The literature of the Old Testament emerges as the deposit of God's revelation of himself to Israel and his journey with them over hundreds of years. The New Testament comes into existence as the deposit of God's climactic revelation of himself in Jesus of Nazareth and the birth of the church. The only record of God writing is of the Ten Commandments. Thus, although God's self-revelation underlies the Bible at every point, the literature of the Bible is written by humans. In order to account for this, we need a model of revelation that takes into account the reality of God's revelation as well as the human role in receiving, recording, and transmitting that revelation. The German theologian Christoph Schwöbel has developed just the sort of model of revelation we need.[2]

In another publication I have used Schwöbel's model to explicate the revelation of God at Sinai (Exod. 19–24).[3] Schwöbel himself applies it to the Christ event, and below, as I explain his model, we will follow him in relating it to the revelation of God in Jesus.

A Model of Revelation

Schwöbel explains that for part of the twentieth century there was a major emphasis on God's action in revelation, and then the pendulum swung to stress the role of human experience in revelation. Both are vital components in revelation, and we need a model that brings them into correct relationship. Schwöbel proposes that we think of revelation as composed of five components:

1. The author of revelation
2. The context of revelation
3. The content of revelation

2. Christoph Schwöbel, *God: Action and Revelation* (Kampen: Kok Pharos, 1992), 83–156.
3. Craig G. Bartholomew, *The God Who Acts in History: The Significance of Sinai* (Grand Rapids: Eerdmans, 2020).

4. The recipient(s) of revelation

5. The result of revelation

One can apply this model to any of God's many revelations of himself. In my opinion, this model particularly comes into its own when applied to the two great riverheads of revelation in the Bible: Sinai in the Old Testament and the Christ event in the New Testament. Following Schwöbel's model, let's unpack the Christ event.

The Author of Revelation

The author of revelation is the trinitarian God, the God who has come to us preeminently in Jesus and thereby revealed himself to us as one God in three persons—Father, Son, and Holy Spirit. God's choice to reveal himself to particular people is grounded in his perfect freedom, and because he is God and humans are creatures, there is an asymmetrical or unequal element to all God's self-revelation to humans. As noted above, the initiative always lies with God. Furthermore, the restrictions of human action do not apply to the divine action of the triune Creator. For example, human action is always bodily, but this restriction does not apply to God. Humans cannot speak without a voice box, but this restriction does not apply to God. If this sounds obvious, you will be surprised to discover how common it is to come across the view in some theologies and biblical studies that God cannot speak because he does not have a body or a voice box!

As fallen humans, who we are and what we will be are often at odds with each other. Not so with God. As Schwöbel says, "There is no difference between intention and act, will and being in God."[4] God, we might say, is perfectly integrated. This means, among many other things, that when we examine God's acts of revelation, we need to remember that they are one with God's acts of creation and redemption. Thus, we need to consider how God's acts of revelation relate to and fit with his acts of creation and redemption. This comes into view immediately in the second aspect of Schwöbel's model.

The Context of Revelation

Unlike God, humans can only be in one place at one time. This means that God's revelation of himself to humans is always situated and contextual;

4. Schwöbel, God, 88.

it cannot be otherwise. God's revelation always takes place within creation and at a particular time and place because this is the nature of the world God has made. This contextual dynamic is sometimes referred to as the medium of revelation; as such, it is a complex entity made up of different elements. Only by being brought together do these elements yield God's self-disclosure.

Because creation is dynamic and "timed," there is always a historical dimension to God's revelation. God's revelation at Sinai takes place in the ancient Near East at Mount Sinai in the late second millennium BC. The major revelation of God in Jesus takes place as a first-century Jew embarks on his public ministry around the age of thirty. Karl Barth captures this well in his comment that God revealed himself in Jewish flesh.[5] Jesus was a first-century Jew, spoke Aramaic, called a group of disciples to accompany him—as rabbis of the time often did—and went around teaching, preaching, and performing miracles in Galilee and Judea, proclaiming that in him the kingdom of God had arrived.

That Jesus was acutely aware of his identity and mission is evident in many ways. One of them is his favorite self-designation: "the Son of Man." This term is almost always found on Jesus's lips in the Gospels and is rarely used of him in the book of Acts and the letters that make up the rest of the New Testament. It seems that Jesus deliberately chose this self-designation to prod his hearers to reflect on just who he is. *Son of Man* has a two-fold background in the Old Testament. As in Ezekiel, it can simply mean a human being with human limitations, but its primary background is in Daniel 7:13–14: "In my vision at night I looked, and there before me was one like a son of man, coming with the clouds of heaven. He approached the Ancient of Days and was led into his presence. He was given authority, glory and sovereign power; all nations and peoples of every language worshiped him. His dominion is an everlasting dominion that will not pass away, and his kingdom is one that will never be destroyed."

It was only when the time had come for Jesus's death that he openly performed and spoke clearly of himself as the Messiah, knowing this would trigger a fatal confrontation with the authorities. Prior to this time, he used the more ambiguous, enigmatic, and indirect term *Son of Man*, a term with all the freight of *Messiah* but indirect, designed to make his hearers stop

---

5. Karl Barth, *Church Dogmatics*, vol. IV/1, *The Doctrine of Reconciliation*, trans. G. W. Bromiley, ed. G. W. Bromiley and T. F. Torrance (Edinburgh: T&T Clark, 1956), 166.

and think. Once he openly presented himself as Messiah in his triumphal entry into Jerusalem on a donkey, Jesus ran afoul of the authorities and was executed brutally by crucifixion, common among the Romans at the time.

As part of the creation, the medium of revelation also has a linguistic element. Jesus taught in Aramaic; the disciples bore witness to him in their preaching and teaching after his death, resurrection, and ascension; and their apostolic witness, recorded in the New Testament, is written in everyday Greek. This witness, as we see in the New Testament, involved far more than just repeating a list of facts; it was the apostolic *interpretation* of what God had done in the Christ event. Paul, for example, unpacks the Christ event in Romans using largely legal metaphors. In an equally long epistle, the author to the Hebrews does the same, but using largely priestly metaphors. Schwöbel thus notes that "the Christ event as the situation of revelation comprises therefore not only the *bruta facta* of the historical sequence of events, but also the claim coming to expression in this series of events (the words, deeds and suffering of Jesus) and the interpretation of both by Jesus' followers."[6]

Both the life of Jesus and the interpretation by his disciples require validation by God. Jesus's life is validated through the resurrection; the witness of the apostles is validated through the work of the Spirit, who validates their witness to their hearers as the truth of their own lives and the whole of reality. The eyewitness testimony of the apostles is enshrined in the documents of the New Testament and becomes the means by which the Spirit leads future generations, and eventually us, into an encounter with God through Jesus.

The Content of Revelation

There can be no question that through revelation God makes known truth about himself. This is often described as propositional revelation. What we must not do is reduce God's self-revelation to propositions. Above all else, through revelation God offers himself just as we might offer ourselves to another person by disclosing ourselves to them. Of course, God is not just another person but the eternal, trinitarian God, and thus while he offers himself truly in a profound act of self-giving, he never offers himself in such a way that we can possess him or know his essence fully. Because

6. Schwöbel, *God*, 88.

he is God, our relationship with him is always appropriately asymmetrical. One way in which this asymmetrical nature shows itself is that God not only makes himself present to us, but he also tells us who he is and what he is doing. We saw this with Moses, and we saw it with Jesus's self-identification as the Son of Man, and we see it in Jesus's ministry as he leads his disciples toward an understanding of who he is. Especially in Jesus's baptism and the transfiguration, we hear the Father identifying Jesus for the disciples as his Son, whom he loves. Jesus did not need the Father to speak about him publicly in this way, but the disciples did and so do we.

A note on commentaries. Christians use an important metaphor to describe the nature of the Bible. We speak of *claritas Scripturae*, the clarity or perspicuity of the Bible as God's Word. This means that the major landmarks of the Bible are clear. For example, you do not need a commentary to tell you that the New Testament is about Jesus or that the New Testament fulfills the Old Testament. However, there is a reverse side to every metaphor, which means in this case that there is much in the Bible that remains unclear. This is one reason we have pastors and teachers and biblical scholars who specialize in the Word so that all of the Bible becomes clearer for God's people in each new generation. At their best, commentaries are an indispensable part of this work, as the history of the church bears eloquent witness. A good commentary is worth its weight in gold, and William Lane's commentary on Mark is one of my favorites.[7]

It is well worth consulting Lane on the baptism of Jesus and the transfiguration in Mark's Gospel. In Mark 1:9–11 we read of Jesus's baptism by John. As Jesus comes up out of the water, the heavens are rent open, and the Spirit descends on Jesus like a dove. A voice comes from heaven: "You are my Son, whom I love; with you I am well pleased." In terms of Jesus's identity and mission this is a rich passage indeed, and Lane helps us unpack it.

Lane notes that the tearing open of heaven (cf. Isa. 64:1), the descent of the Spirit, and the Father's testimony from heaven all bear witness to the cosmic significance of Jesus's mission. Just as the Israelites had to be consecrated in Exodus 19 before God would descend on Mount Sinai, so it is that after Jesus's consecration to his mission on behalf of sinners through his baptism, the Spirit descends on him, signifying that his mission is that

7. William L. Lane, *The Gospel of Mark*, New International Commentary on the New Testament (Grand Rapids: Eerdmans, 1974).

of a new exodus (cf. Isa. 32:15; 44:3; 63:10–14). The Spirit descending like a dove may allude to Genesis 1:2, where the Spirit of God hovers over the as-yet-unformed creation, thus showing us that Jesus's new exodus will usher in a new creation. It could also be a symbol of Israel, thus identifying Jesus as the true Israelite. The Father's voice from heaven validates Jesus and his mission unequivocally. It likely contains multiple allusions to the Old Testament, to verses such as Genesis 22:2; Psalm 2:7; and Isaiah 42:1. As must we, the Father uses the Old Testament to explain the significance of what is happening in the mission of Jesus. *Son* refers to Jesus's divinity. Lane notes that "the rending of the heavens, the descent of the Spirit and the declaration of God do not alter Jesus' essential status, but serve to indicate the cosmic significance of Jesus' submission to the Servant-vocation and affirm God's good pleasure in his Son."[8]

In the narrative of Jesus's transfiguration (Mark 9:2–13), we again hear the Father's voice from heaven: "This is my Son, whom I love. Listen to him!" (v. 7). Jesus's fulfillment of the Old Testament is evoked by the presence of Moses (the Law) and Elijah (the Prophets). Peter is overcome by the transfiguration, and his misunderstanding of Jesus's mission is instructive for us. He is so impressed by what has happened that he proposes building three shelters on the mount, one each for Moses, Elijah, and Jesus. Luke's account of the transfiguration provides us with more detail than Mark's, and one detail in particular helps us understand why Peter got the transfiguration so very wrong. Luke tells us that Moses and Elijah discussed with Jesus his coming "departure" (Luke 9:31). The Greek word here is *exodos*, alerting us to the fact that Jesus must descend from the mount and continue his mission, because he is not just leading slaves out of Egypt but leading the whole creation in an exodus from sin and death.

In Jesus's baptism and transfiguration, God is disclosed to us—as Father, Son, and Spirit. Jesus's ministry is validated by the Father, and through his speech the Father interprets for the disciples and us what is going on. In all of this we can see *God's self-identification* in his revelation. Because God's revelation is personal, it is also particular, to the ancient Near Eastern Israelites in the Old Testament and to Jesus's disciples and followers in the New Testament. However, although it is historically particular, it is universal or cosmic in its scope, revealing the truth about ourselves and

8. Lane, *Gospel of Mark*, 58.

our world and about God's purpose in Jesus of recovering his reign over his creation and leading it toward that destiny for which he always intended.

The Recipient(s) of Revelation

Although God's revelation is asymmetrical, for it to be successful it has to be received by those particular, historical persons to whom it is addressed. If Israel had not listened to God and entered into a covenant relationship with him mediated by Moses, we would not know about God's revelation at Sinai. The same goes for the Christ event. The disciples needed willingly to follow Jesus, to grow and develop in their understanding of him, to come to see him as and confess him to be the Messiah, and to live through his death, resurrection, and ascension, so that after Pentecost they could bear truthful witness to the Christ event. It is often noted that Peter's response to Jesus's leading question "Who do you say I am?"—namely, "You are the Messiah" (Mark 8:29)—marks a turning point in the Gospels, as Jesus turns toward the cross that awaits him. Had the disciples not done any of this, we would have no New Testament.

There is thus a major human dimension to God's revelation, and we ignore it at our peril. Because it is historical and concrete, God's revelation is received, interpreted, and passed on by particular human beings in particular, historical contexts. Knowing that the Old Testament is written in Hebrew and Aramaic and the New Testament in Greek, this should be obvious to us, but it is easily missed. The printing press was only invented hundreds of years after the Christ event, and so we need to recognize that the transmission of God's revelation took place according to the technical possibilities of the ages in which it was given.

It is often hard to be precise about the process by which the books of the Bible came into existence. Take the Pentateuch, for example. Moses is the central human figure in Exodus–Deuteronomy, and there are indeed times when Moses is instructed by God to write things down. However, Deuteronomy records Moses's death, and presumably this was not written by Moses. And, of course, Moses does not feature in Genesis at all. Thus, although a case can and should be made for the Pentateuch being substantially Mosaic, clearly it came into existence over time, with unknown scribes and editors playing an important role. It is possible that parts of the Pentateuch—for example, the stories of Abraham, Isaac, and Jacob in Genesis 12–50—were passed on orally for generations before being committed to writing. It is also clear that those who recorded these narratives thought long and hard about them, incorporating into the telling of the stories profound interpretation of what God was doing.

When it comes to the Christ event, we have not one but four Gospels. Each tells the story of Jesus, majoring on the three years of his public ministry in its own complementary way. The first three Gospels, often called the Synoptic Gospels because they can fairly easily be seen and examined together, use repeatedly the language of the kingdom of God/heaven. John's Gospel, on the other hand, uses this language rarely and has its own vocabulary for evoking the eschatological reality of the Christ event.

In the thirteen letters of Paul, we listen in on one side of a correspondence between Paul and the churches or with his coleaders. In Romans Paul expands the genre of a letter to explain in great detail the Christ event for the church in Rome. As noted above, he does this using primarily legal metaphors. In Hebrews the author opens up the depth of the Christ event by using priestly metaphors. Hebrews and Paul's Letters demonstrate the minds of first-rate theologians, immersed in the Old Testament, who reflected long and hard about what God had done in Jesus. The same is true of the other letters in the New Testament and the extraordinary book with which the Bible ends, Revelation.

The human dimension of revelation is thus very real, and it is one reason why study of the cultures in which God's revelation was given is so instructive. God's revelation is historical, and the more we learn about the historical contexts in which it was given, the clearer it becomes. Familiarity with Hebrew and Greek, ancient Near Eastern and Greco-Roman culture, and intertestamental Judaism provides vital tools in the toolbox of biblical scholars. This is all exceedingly hard work, far more than one person can do alone, but it is work we should welcome because it reminds us that God did not reveal himself by dropping the Bible from heaven. Rather, he immersed himself in the life of ancient Near Eastern Israel and in the first-century-AD Christ event. His revelation was received, reduced to writing, passed on, and eventually translated into English for us today.

The Result of Revelation

The result of revelation is, according to Schwöbel, faith. Faith is a rich biblical and theological concept. It is made possible by God's action but exercised as such by humans. Schwöbel defines it as "the *existential relation* of unconditional trust in God as he discloses himself in the medium of the Gospel of Christ."[9] *Existential* is a good word for faith because although faith includes knowledge about God, it is a response to an encounter with God and thus a living relationship of trust, obedience or submission, and belief.

Trust and belief in God, as he discloses himself to us in Jesus, are no small thing. We saw above how the Father validates Jesus at his baptism and transfiguration. When we come to faith, we share with the Father in that affirmation about Jesus: he is the Son of God, he is the one whom the Father loves, and we will listen to him. While faith is always personal and particular—think of "I believe . . ." in the Apostles' Creed—the object of faith, the triune God, means that faith opens out onto the whole of creation, because the triune God is the Creator and Redeemer. Faith means that we understand ourselves as God sees us—his creatures made in his image—and we understand our world as God's creation. We might say that faith orients us toward the world in a particular way or, alternatively, that it yields a worldview. Because God is the Creator, Lord, King, Redeemer, and Savior, the origin and telos of all, faith in him has consequences for all of life, including our view of the nature of reality (ontology) and how we go about knowing the world truly (epistemology).

Faith has important implications for how we approach the Bible. Again and again one hears how a person's response to the Bible changed once they came to faith. The Bible witnesses to the God who has come to us in Jesus, and invariably faith is accompanied by a sense that the record of God's revelation of himself in the Bible can be trusted. We become like the early Christians, who devoted themselves to the teaching of the apostles precisely because it was in and through that teaching that they encountered Jesus. There is something appropriately circular about this logic since the initiative in revelation always remains with God and not with us. There are undoubtedly many good reasons for believing the Bible to be God's Word, but such arguments can only take us so far. They cannot usher us into a living relationship with God, which is what the Bible is intended for. This depends on the work of the Spirit, opening our eyes and our ears to receive the gift of God again and again. As part of God's self-revelation, the Bible is in this respect self-authenticating.

9. Schwöbel, *God*, 96.

The Formation of the Canon

Historically, discussions of the canon of Scripture have centered around two issues: the *terminus a quo* and the *terminus ad quem*, the time from which the canon emerged and the time at which it was closed. As confidence in revelation has been lost or marginalized, much of the debate has come to focus on the latter question. What we have seen in this chapter, however, is that we simply cannot understand the emergence of the canon correctly if we do not take God's self-disclosure seriously. It is God's revelation of himself to Old Testament Israel and preeminently in the Christ event that underlies the canon of the Bible and makes it possible at all. God's revelation of himself at Sinai and the explosion of good news in the Christ event generate the writings that become the sixty-six books of the Bible. Once we see this, the focus of the emergence of the canon shifts from being a question of when the community declared the canon closed to the question of its recognition by God's people. Rather than casting their vote, the people recognized which literature faithfully and truly witnesses to God's revelation in history.

At the same time, I have stressed above the human role in the production of the Bible. Scholars have proposed many hypotheses about how the different books came into existence, but again we cannot be sure. With the emergence of historical criticism in biblical studies in the late nineteenth century, it became common to identify four major sources underlying the Pentateuch—namely, JEDP—and to this day many scholars devote enormous energy to identifying and reconstructing these sources. More recently, some scholars have stressed that we need to understand how books were composed in the ancient Near East, which would provide some degree of control for theories of book production among the Israelites. Substantial work is emerging on how Israelite scribes may have edited and transmitted texts, and such work is likely to change our understanding of the formation of Old Testament books for the better. God's revelation of himself is unique in the ancient Near East and in the Greco-Roman world, so we need to be prepared for important differences between the Bible and comparative literature. Nevertheless, this turn to comparative analyses of the production of books is constructive, and at the very least it raises important questions. It has often been assumed, for example, that long periods of oral transmission lay behind the books of the Old Testament, with scores of anonymous scribes and editors leaving their mark on the final form of the text. Marc Van De Mieroop, however, observes that in Babylon, writing was privileged over speech and oral transmission and that texts were written from the start.[10] Thus, our understanding of how Old Testament texts developed is in flux and may remain so for some time.

We have anchored the question of the canon in the *terminus a quo*. Nevertheless, the *terminus ad quem* remains important. Not surprisingly, when it comes to the closure of the Old and New Testament canons, there is disagreement among scholars. In my view, there is strong evidence to support the closure of the Old Testament canon well before the time of Jesus and the apostles. Ben Sira wrote Ecclesiasticus in the early second century BC. His grandson translated it into Greek, and in the prologue he refers to his grandfather as a student of "the Law and the Prophets and the other books" (NRSV). It is highly probable that he is referring here to the typical Jewish tripartite structure of the Old Testament—namely, the Law, the Prophets, and the Writings.[11] Similarly, Josephus, writing in the last ten years of the first century AD, refers to twenty-two books making up the Hebrew Bible in three parts, which is probably the same collection we have today, with the possible exception of one book.[12] For Josephus this is no new canon but one that has long been recognized. Many details of the formation of the Old Testament canon remain elusive, but there is no reason to question that it was closed well before the time of Jesus.

Unlike the Old Testament, the New Testament came into existence in a relatively short and concentrated period of time. The canon of the New Testament was only formally closed around the fourth to fifth centuries AD, but its core was taken by the early church to be authoritative very early on, and it remained, with time, for the church to discern precisely which books were genuinely apostolic and catholic.

Conclusion

The exchange between the reader of the Bible and the congregation—"This is the Word of the Lord," and "Thanks be to God"—serves as a powerful re-

10. Marc Van De Mieroop, *Philosophy before the Greeks: The Pursuit of Truth in Ancient Babylonia* (Princeton: Princeton University Press, 2016).

11. See F. F. Bruce, *The Canon of Scripture* (Downers Grove, IL: InterVarsity, 1988), 31; E. Earle Ellis, *The Old Testament in Early Christianity: Canon and Interpretation in the Light of Modern Research* (Tübingen: Mohr, 1991), 39–40; Roger T. Beckwith, *The Old Testament Canon of the New Testament Church and Its Background in Early Judaism* (Grand Rapids: Eerdmans, 1986), 110–11.

12. See Beckwith, *Old Testament Canon*, 78–80; Bruce, *Canon of Scripture*, 32–34.

minder of what is at stake in the canonicity of the Bible. Underlying the Bible and at its origin is the revelation of the living God. Canonicity draws our attention to the fact that these sixty-six books, made up of the Old Testament and the New Testament, are a fully trustworthy witness to God's self-revelation. Because God is God, his self-revelation explains who we are, the nature of the world in which we live, what history is about, and where it will all conclude. There are some differences between Protestants, Catholics, and Orthodox Christians about the number of books in the Old Testament canon, but all groups accept these sixty-six books as inspired and authoritative. We never worship the Bible, but we trust it to provide us with an infallible and thus fully trustworthy witness to the triune God and his purposes in his world. Indeed, it is the Bible that the Spirit uses in particular to invite us again and again to encounter the living God and to receive the gift of God himself.

DISCUSSION QUESTIONS

1. Can you remember your first Bible? What version was it?
2. What translation do you most like to use now? Why?
3. A long journey precedes the Bible arriving in your hands. How would you explain to a friend how we got the Bible?
4. Revelation is central to the origin of the Bible. Can you recall the main elements in Schwöbel's model of revelation?
5. See if you can elaborate on God's revelation at Sinai or in the Christ event using Schwöbel's categories.
6. Why did Jesus favor the title "the Son of Man"? What is its Old Testament background, and how does this help us understand its meaning?

FURTHER READING

Bavinck, Herman. *Reformed Dogmatics*. Vol. 1, *Prolegomena*, edited by John Bolt, translated by John Vriend. Grand Rapids: Baker Academic, 2003. See especially part IV on revelation.

Beckwith, Roger T. *The Old Testament Canon of the New Testament Church and Its Background in Early Judaism*. Grand Rapids: Eerdmans, 1986.

Bruce, F. F. *The Canon of Scripture*. Downers Grove, IL: InterVarsity, 1988.

Ellis, E. Earle. *The Old Testament in Early Christianity: Canon and Interpretation in the Light of Modern Research*. Tübingen: Mohr, 1991.

Moule, C. F. D. *The Origin of Christology*. Cambridge: Cambridge University Press, 1977. See especially pages 11–22. Moule has a very useful discussion of "the Son of Man."

DEVOTIONAL EXERCISE

1. Amid your work and activities, slow down and come to stillness before God. Savor five minutes of just being before him and with him.

2. In your reading of this book, are you feeling drawn toward God or away from him? Reflect on how you feel and tell God about it.

3. Read through the following passage slowly, several times.

   1 John 1:1–4
   That which was from the beginning, which we have heard, which we have seen with our eyes, which we have looked at and our hands have touched—this we proclaim concerning the Word of life. The life appeared; we have seen it and testify to it, and we proclaim to you the eternal life, which was with the Father and has appeared to us. We proclaim to you what we have seen and heard, so that you also may have fellowship with us. And our fellowship is with the Father and with his Son, Jesus Christ. We write this to make our joy complete.

   Take note of anything that catches your attention in this passage.
   What do you learn about Jesus?
   Reflect on how this eyewitness testimony has come to you today.
   Reflect on the goal, the telos, of this testimony.

4. Take several minutes to enjoy being present to God, sharing in fellowship with the Father and the Son through the Spirit.

5. Imagine Jesus sitting in a chair next to you. Tell him what you have learned about him from this passage. Thank him.

6. Conclude your time with this prayer:

> Glory be to the Father and to the Son and to the Holy Spirit, as it was in the beginning, is now, and shall be forevermore. Amen.

SUGGESTED ACTIVITIES

1. Hold your Bible in your hands. Take note of its cover, the font, and any other characteristics of it. In your imagination trace the journey of your Bible back to its origins in God's revelation.

2. Ask some of your friends or family how they think we got the Bible. Compare their answers with what you have learned from this chapter.

4

A TRIADIC APPROACH

The Motivation for Studying the Bible

Think of a historical or contemporary person you admire a great deal who has had a major influence on your life, though you know little about them. Now imagine you discovered a book in which they revealed themself to you in detail. How would you respond? Of course, you would be very excited, and you would devote yourself to reading and studying the book in order to learn everything you could about this person. You would return to it again and again, consulting other sources where relevant—anything to help you understand better the person revealed in the book.

It is the same with the Bible but to a much greater extent. A helpful way to think of the Bible is as a field in which is hidden the pearl of great price—namely, Jesus. This draws, of course, on Jesus's parable of a treasure hidden in a field. As Jesus says, one would sell everything in order to buy the field and access the treasure. Of course, one would first need to come to value this treasure above everything else. This is why our fascination with the Bible generally follows on from conversion. Through conversion we are awakened to the overwhelming reality of God, who has come to us in Jesus and invites us into a personal relationship with him. We start to see that God is the great treasure of life, and that it is worth giving up everything in order to have him as God and Father.

But how do you access him? How do you receive more and more of him? John reminds us that no one has ever seen God, but Jesus has made him known (John 1:18). What we need, therefore, is Jesus. But how will we access him? The first Christians, converted after Peter's powerful sermon on the day of Pentecost, knew the answer; they devoted themselves to the teaching of the apostles (Acts 2:42). The lives of these early Christians had been turned upside down by the coming of the Spirit at Pentecost, and they had been converted. Now they longed for more, far more, of Jesus. They devoted themselves to the apostles' teaching because they knew it was there they would find what they were looking for.

Jesus deliberately appointed twelve disciples to be with him during his public ministry. They were profoundly formed by these three years with Jesus, but more than that, they were eyewitnesses of his life and deeds and thus were in a unique position to bear authoritative witness about him. In one way or another, it is their witness about Jesus that makes up the New Testament. And, of course, the Jesus we find in their witness affirms unequivocally the authority of the Old Testament, and so it inevitably accompanies the testimony of the apostles.

This is why we read and study the Bible—because it is in and through this book that we find Jesus, and he reveals God to us. Especially when you study church history, you discover that Jews (the Hebrew Bible, Old Testament) and Christians have been doing this for hundreds of years. In the process they have bequeathed to us a vast amount of literature containing their reflections on the Bible, part of what we refer to as the Jewish-Christian tradition. Until about two hundred years ago, finding and learning about God remained the great motivation for studying the Bible. It is only comparatively recently that the motivation for biblical studies underwent a significant shift. Today you cannot study the Bible without this shift affecting you, for better and for worse. Thus, an indispensable tool for studying the Bible today is an awareness of the history of modern biblical study.

A History of Four Turns

Modernity as the Context

All of us live in the modern world, a product of what is called modernity. This is the air we breathe and is as natural to us as the water in which a fish swims. Driving a car, taking a flight, going under anesthetic, squeezing out multicolored toothpaste, making a phone call, switching on a computer, voting—all of these and so much more are the products of modernity. What we often fail to realize is that modernity is a comparatively recent development, sparked after the Renaissance by the scientific, philosophical, and historical revolutions of the Enlightenment in the seventeenth and eighteenth centuries. The Enlightenment led to a reformation of Western culture from the ground up, bringing with it huge advances and radical changes. Many of these are good. We would not want to undergo an operation without anesthetic! However, as modernity began to unravel (a name for this is "postmodernism") in the twentieth century—the century that many regard as the most brutal in history—it became increasingly apparent that not all of modernity was as benign as thought.

Why does this matter to us? It matters because modernity fundamentally reshaped how we do academic studies. The Enlightenment was rightly concerned that academic studies should yield truth, but its methods for getting there marked a substantial shift. Prior to the Enlightenment, a Christian understanding of the world could largely be assumed, and academic studies were pursued within such a framework. The radical wing of the Enlightenment, which became the dominant one, challenged this view to the core, arguing that human autonomy, not God, should be the touchstone for any academic quest for truth.

This approach, which in the West allowed for freedom of religion but also resulted in privatized religion, sought to exclude religion from the great public spheres of life, including education—and thus biblical studies. Students were free to be religious and to practice religion in their private lives, but religious commitments should be left at the door when seeking truth in academia. With time, this yielded an approach to biblical interpretation known as historical criticism. If, for example, you take a course on the Pentateuch, you will encounter JEDP, the four main sources that historical critics identify in the Pentateuch. The idea was, as in all other disciplines, to study the Bible objectively and scientifically through the lens of the modern worldview, in order to arrive at the truth about it.

Rigorous historical-critical study of the Bible has now been underway for a good 150 years. It has produced a great deal of value. Every part of the Bible has been scrutinized with exceptional thoroughness, yielding many vital insights. Our knowledge of the cultures around Israel has also increased exponentially, so that today major sources from the ancient Near East and the Greco-Roman world are available to help us understand the Bible far better.

The more we know about the cultures in which the Bible came into existence, the better. This flows directly from how we received the Bible. The Bible emerges from God's deep involvement with an ancient Near Eastern nation, Israel, and from his action in the Christ event. The Bible did not drop from heaven but comes to us as a result of God's actions in history. This is obvious, but in case you need any persuasion, think of the languages in which it is written: the Old Testament is in Hebrew with small portions in Aramaic, and the New Testament is written in Koine Greek of the first century AD. Of course, we all benefit from translations in our own languages, but they are just that: translations. Study the Bible seriously, and you will soon start wondering if you should study Hebrew and Greek so you can read the Bible in its original languages. The answer is, of course, you should if you have the opportunity.

We can and should confess the clarity of the Bible, *claritas Scripturae*, meaning that the major truths of the Bible are on its surface and readily understood. However, "clarity" here is a metaphor, and as such it alerts us to two things: first, the major elements of the Bible are readily understood, and second, there is much in the Bible in every generation that is unclear. This is why we have pastors and teachers to help us grasp and be grasped by the whole counsel of God. Scholars and our knowledge of the cultures of the Bible all have roles to play in helping us understand the Bible more clearly.

However, the legacy of historical criticism has been ambiguous at best. It promised assured results, but these have never been achieved. Furthermore, it endlessly fragmented the Bible, separating the New Testament from the Old and then dividing up each Testament into more and more—apparently irreconcilable—fragments. All of this makes it almost impossible to receive the Bible as the unified Word of God it claims to be and to embrace it with the same excitement that led to our studies in the first place. In the process it has become clear that the place from which you study the Bible—your starting point—is not neutral. If you start with autonomous human reason, excluding the very possibility of divine action in the world, this will shape the questions you ask, the methods you use, and the results you reach.

A choice must be made at the outset. Am I approaching the world I wish to investigate as God's good, fallen-but-being-redeemed creation, or am I approaching it as a random product of an ungoverned evolutionary process? And of these two lenses, which will I use for studying the Bible? Fortunately, in recent decades we have witnessed a remarkable flourishing of Christian philosophy, and luminaries such as Alvin Plantinga have argued that the Christian scholar is entirely warranted in approaching the Bible as God's Word and doing rigorous scholarship within such a paradigm. This does not for a moment mean ignoring the insights yielded from historical criticism, but it does mean doing the hard work of separating such insights from their presuppositions and resituating them within a Christian perspective. In order to do this, we need a handle on the way in which modern biblical interpretation developed, and in this respect it is helpful to think of four turns: the historical, the literary, the postmodern, and the theological.

The Historical Turn

Although its roots are much earlier, historical criticism was the dominant mode of biblical interpretation in mainstream biblical studies by the early twentieth century. Its overarching concern with history is embedded in its name. History had become a major discipline in the modern university, and historical criticism sought to scrutinize the Bible through the lens of modern historical method.

In light of the neutrality postulate of modernity, the Bible had to be read like any other ancient text. From this perspective the surface of the text is full of divine action, which a scientific approach cannot take seriously. Thus, historical criticism repeatedly sought to penetrate below the surface of the text to the history—understood in modern terms—underlying it. Four major methods emerged: source criticism, which attempted to identify and reconstruct the sources behind the Bible (e.g., JEDP for the Pentateuch); form criticism, which sought to identify the smallest identifiable, cohesive unit in a text and then trace its form from its life setting in ancient Israel or the early church; tradition criticism, which identified major themes or traditions in the Bible (e.g., Zion) and then sought to trace the development of such traditions; and redaction criticism, which aimed to analyze the role of editors in bringing books to their final shape.

There are varieties of historical criticism and developments within it, but at its extreme, historical criticism "discovered" layer upon layer in biblical texts. Furthermore, without God in the picture, human and historical agency were overemphasized. For the Gospels, for example, a trend developed of seeing them as the products of particular communities, and then the focus became excavating and describing these individual communities. Redaction criticism was interesting because it brought the totality of each individual book back into the picture, a concern that would move front and center with the literary turn described below.

As historical criticism came to dominate mainstream biblical studies, Christian scholars reacted in different ways. Some aligned themselves with the neutrality postulate of modernity and sought to arrive at more conservative results using the same methods. This is James Barr's great criticism of evangelicals in his *Fundamentalism*; you always know where such scholars will arrive or land![1] Others recognized the challenge of historical criticism to any kind of recognizable biblical history and put all their energy into defending the historicity of the Bible. What was often missing was a sense that a Christian perspective might reconceive the project of biblical studies in a way that could receive the insights of historical criticism but develop in its own way with its own priorities.

The Literary Turn

In the 1970s historical criticism was shaken up by a rediscovery of the Bible as literature. Certainly, in Old Testament studies, this move came primarily from Jewish literary scholars such as Robert Alter and Meir Sternberg. The literary turn reminded us that biblical texts are literature and that we access their meaning through the poetics—that is, the literary devices—of the text. Ancient Israelite and New Testament authors operated with a sophisticated poetics, and the analysis of the books of the Bible and parts thereof along literary lines challenged many of the key elements in historical criticism. For example, if a story in a book or corpus is paralleled by a similar story, historical critics spoke of "doublets," indicating different sources. A literary approach brought to the very same data a very different possibility—namely, that of deliberate repetition, a major characteristic of literature. In countless such ways, the literary turn challenged historical

1. James Barr, *Fundamentalism*, 2nd ed. (London: SCM, 1981).

criticism and opened up fresh ways of reading biblical books with nuance and depth. This was also a time when other challenges to historical criticism were emerging, but before the literary challenge could be fully appropriated and appreciated, postmodernism arrived in the 1980s, casting its shadow far and wide.

The Postmodern Turn

At the beginning of the twentieth century, the spirit of modernity was utopian in its hope for what autonomous, scientific rationality could achieve. By the end of this extraordinarily brutal century, it was uncertain if modernity would survive. Multiple crises led to the unraveling of modernity's DNA, and fundamental questions about modernity itself emerged. These probing questions addressed the very possibility of truth, the validity of metanarratives or grand stories about the world, science and reason, and what it means to be human. In the wake of modernity came postmodernity.

If modernity championed the right method as the key to arriving at the truth, postmodernism celebrated a wild pluralism of an endless variety of methods. Postmodernism began in literary studies and then spread to almost every other discipline, including biblical studies. Whereas historical-critical and literary readings had been the norm at mainstream conferences, now a bewildering variety engulfed biblical studies: deconstructionist readings, a range of ideological readings, the application of a variety of especially French theories to the Bible, new historicist readings, post-Marxist readings, and so on. It seemed that the more creative things one could do with biblical texts, the better.

Postmodernism's attack on method as the route to truth was penetrating, but it remained within the overarching modern paradigm of human autonomy. The casualty was truth—and in the case of biblical studies, the possibility and goal of truthful readings of the Bible. The result was that the postmodern turn in biblical studies was deconstructive rather than constructive, and as postmodernism has waned, historical criticism has remained the default mode of much mainstream biblical studies. Another result of postmodernism is that its pluralism opened the door to religious readings of the Bible. The logic was hard to deny. If an endless variety of readings is acceptable and there is no right method, then there is no reason to exclude overtly religious readings. A result of this was a renaissance in theological interpretation of the Bible.

The Theological Turn

Theological interpretation is all about reading the Bible as Scripture for the church. As we noted above, this has a long and distinguished pedigree. The father of modern theological interpretation is Karl Barth. In my early theological studies, I learned that Barth was a liberal to be avoided, but we never actually read Barth. Years later I read large parts of his *Church Dogmatics* and was shocked to discover how rich it is, not least in terms of biblical interpretation. His writing is filled with detailed exegesis in the service of theology for the church. To give one example, *Church Dogmatics* contains some one hundred pages of small-font, wonderfully rich, theological exegesis of Genesis 1:1–2:4a. There are, of course, significant issues over which I as an evangelical disagree with Barth, but his contribution was immense, and he almost singlehandedly toppled the liberal theology of his day. Historically, I cannot think of a single theologian who does as much biblical exegesis as Barth.

Brevard Childs studied under Barth and then devoted his career to the development of his canonical hermeneutic for biblical studies. Childs focused on developing a method that considered the Bible as the authoritative canon for the Christian church. His approach yielded a rich corpus of literature. By the end of the twentieth century, a minority renaissance of theological interpretation was underway, with dictionaries, commentary series, and articles following this approach.

Theological interpretation is a broad tent that holds a variety of perspectives. The possibilities it presents need to be seized but only as a means to recover an integrated, holistic hermeneutic for the Bible. What might this look like?

A Triadic Approach

One way to treat theological interpretation is simply as another method among many others for reading the Bible. This is a mistake. At its best, theological interpretation gets at the foundational issues in biblical studies, reminding us not just *for whom* we read the Bible but *from where* we do so. As Proverbs 1:7 says, "The fear of the LORD is the beginning of knowledge";

our starting point in the quest for wisdom and understanding makes all the difference, including when it comes to reading the Bible. From where should we begin and continue when we engage in biblical studies? With the fear of YHWH.

"The fear of YHWH" is rich with significance. YHWH is the name of God particularly associated with his rescue of his people from slavery in Egypt and his establishment of them as his people at Sinai (Exod. 19–Num. 10). Thus, the name YHWH evokes God as the Redeemer who brings his people to himself (Exod. 19:4). However, as made clear by the Sinai narrative and Genesis 2–3 (cf. the unusual name of God, "YHWH Elohim," in these chaps.), YHWH is no local deity but the Creator of heaven and earth. "Fear of" refers to the reverence appropriate to this God, akin to the hallowing of God's name in the Lord's Prayer. Wisdom and understanding are gained when we make reverence for this God our starting point and the foundation in our quest for knowledge and wisdom. Faith in God and trust in the Bible as his Word yield a very particular orientation toward ourselves and the world, what we might call a Christian worldview. We will be wise interpreters of the Bible if we indwell this worldview and allow it to shape all of our life, including our exegesis.

This may sound simplistic or easy, but it is neither. It certainly means that prayer should accompany all our work, and it certainly means that trust in the Bible as God's fully trustworthy Word is vital. But it involves far more than that. Let me explain.

I will argue that, rather than seeing historical, literary, and theological approaches to the Bible as separate endeavors, we need an integrated hermeneutic that includes all three. However, when we start to talk about each of these dimensions, we find not only that they are complex but that very different answers exist for basic questions like, What is literature? What is history?

Inevitably, since humans produce literature and write history (historiography), such questions take us to even more foundational ones: What does it mean to be human (anthropology)? How do we know the world truthfully (epistemology)? What is the nature of our world (ontology or metaphysics)? In other words, beneath the historical, the literary, and the kerygmatic are deep philosophical and theological issues. And once again, there is a diversity of views about these foundational issues. Digging even deeper, we move from philosophy and theology into worldview, since it is worldview that orients each person toward the world and yields a phi-losophy and a theology.[2]

Thus, allowing our worldview to shape our interpretation will mean thinking very hard about history, literature, and theology so that we de-velop a hermeneutic for the Bible that is of one piece with the view of the world yielded by the Bible. Fortunately, we are now heirs of generations of scholars—in many cases, centuries of scholars—who have done hard work in these areas and whose work we can use to our advantage.

The Historical Dimension

In one sense, we and the Bible are historical. We are embedded in his-tory, and the Bible comes to us in foreign languages and from cultures very different from our own. The Bible is historical because it emerges from and tells the story of God's engagement with ancient Near Eastern Israel, climaxing in the Christ event. Large parts of the Bible tell us about what happened, and their truthfulness depends upon the events they narrate having actually taken place. Of course, this is by no means true of everything in the Bible. For example, neither the Psalms, nor Prov-erbs, nor the letters of the New Testament are historical narrative, so their connection with historical events is lessened. However, much of the Bible is historical narrative, and we need to read the Bible with this in mind.

However, the historical dimension intertwines with the literary and the theological, and we must bear this in mind even as we take the histori-cal dimension seriously. For example, it would be wrong to describe the Bible simply as a history book. Ancient history writing (cf. Herodotus) and modern history writing alike set out to tell the story of events and periods as accurately as possible. While events are central to biblical historical narrative, its aim is different—that is, to confront us with the God at work in these events and to call us to follow and obey him. In 1 and 2 Kings, for example, a great deal about the reign of each king is omitted because the narrator is most interested in how the kings related to YHWH. King Omri is glossed over as a bad king, whereas we know from external sources that

2. On worldview see Michael W. Goheen and Craig G. Bartholomew, *Living at the Crossroads: An Introduction to Christian Worldview* (Grand Rapids: Baker Academic, 2008).

his cultural and economic achievements were huge. However, these are simply not what the narrator is interested in. So, too, with the Gospels. Scholars have struggled to pin down just what type of literature they are because they largely focus on the three years of Jesus's public ministry, omitting most of his life. Clearly, they are not biographical in the modern sense of the term.

The Literary Dimension

Narrative in the term *historical narrative* points us to the Bible's literary dimension. In literature, narrative can be historical or fictional. For example, in Lord of the Rings, J. R. R. Tolkien's masterpiece, one can reflect on its characteristics as literature: the introduction of the main characters in their setting (the Shire), the problem being faced, the way in which the plot unfolds—often moving back and forward to different characters and times—characterization and character development, the speeches and songs, and the final climax of the story following a long journey. Of course, as extraordinary as Lord of the Rings is, Tolkien knew, as do we, that he was creating a fictional world. Indeed, the difference between fictional narrative and historical narrative is located in what the author aims to do. Historical narrative aims to tell us, however badly or well, about things that actually happened and people who actually lived. It attempts to represent the past accurately.

Both historical narrative and fictional narrative are forms of narrative. In recent decades scholars have observed that both use the same range of devices, or poetics, in order to tell their story. It is not possible to distinguish the two from their poetics alone. It is the intent of the author that distinguishes the one from the other. Furthermore, although historical narrative means to represent the past accurately, it never merely holds up a mirror to the past, which is impossible. To define history as what happened in the past is woefully inadequate, especially when it comes to history writing. Millions of things take place every second, and thus history writing is always selective, focusing on aspects of reality, on particular people, and so on which it regards as vital for a particular understanding of the past or the events under consideration.

How then does being aware of the literary nature of the Bible help us read it? In myriad ways. We need to notice the poetics at work in biblical books—things like the unfolding plot, the repetition, the key characters and their characterization, the division of the story into different acts and scenes. Fictional narrative requires a suspension of belief since it creates a world that is not tethered to history in the same way as historical narrative. Historical narrative may not require this, but any engagement with narrative does require a developed imagination. Old Testament Israel was a culture of masterful storytellers, and if we are to hear the narratives of the Bible with the full and rich range of their acoustics, we have to enter into the narratives imaginatively.

Neither Psalms nor Proverbs is historical narrative, but they are literature and similarly require a deeply engaged imagination if they are to be fully received. Scholars disagree on the historical nature of some Old Testament books. Jonah is clearly a masterful narrative, but does it intend to tell us about events that actually happened? Although Job is full of very long and repetitive speeches, it has an overarching narrative shape. However, the speeches are written not as prose but as poetry. Similarly, there is a debate about whether Qoheleth (the Preacher in Ecclesiastes) is Solomon or a fictional character like Solomon. This highlights an important point: something is not less true because it is fictional.

I grew up in apartheid South Africa, a society in which racial discrimination was legally imposed on every aspect of life: where we could live, schools we could attend, sports clubs we could join, whether we could vote. Not far from where I grew up in KwaZulu Natal lived a strong government opponent and author. Alan Paton wrote a remarkable novel, *Cry, the Beloved Country*.[3] In its own fictional way, this novel tells the truth about apartheid South Africa. Astonishingly, it was never banned, unlike so many other books. I think this was because it was a novel, and the apartheid government could not imagine that a novel could be so powerful. Alas, some evangelicals are like this—they think that something can only be true if it is historical. However, if Jonah and Job are not historical in the sense of aiming to tell us about real people and events accurately, they are still exceptionally powerful vehicles for the message they convey. A problem arises with such books being fictional only if they mean to be telling us about what actually happened, such that their message depends upon the events' historicity.

3. Alan Paton, *Cry, the Beloved Country* (New York: Scribner, 1948).

The Theological Dimension

Theological refers to the "God-speak" dimension of biblical books. It is not my preferred term for this dimension because it has at least two major meanings. On the one hand, *theological* refers us back to the foundational aspects we discussed above: a worldview with the trinitarian God at the center. On the other hand, *theological* refers to the fact that the books of the Bible always carry a message about God, the world, and us in relation to God. My preference is to use the term *kerygmatic*—message, proclamation—for this dimension. *Kērygma* is the Greek word for message, and attending to the message is above all what we are after when we read the Bible.

If we think of these three dimensions—historical, literary, and kerygmatic —and their interrelationship in the Bible, an important insight emerges. In the Bible the kerygmatic dimension dominates. History and literature are fundamental ingredients but always in service of the kerygma. We cannot access the kerygma of the text apart from the historical dimensions and its poetics, but we fall short if we fail to make our goal to hear what God is saying to us today through the kerygma, the message of the text. Let me give you some examples of why this is so important.

Take the book of Kings. Historical analysis concerns itself with whether these kings existed, the times during which they reigned, whether they were northern or southern kings, what we can know about their reigns from Kings and extrabiblical material, and so on. When historical criticism brought so much of biblical history into question, evangelicals understand-ably mounted a vigorous defense of the Bible's historicity. You will see this in the evangelical commentaries from the mid- to late-twentieth century, for example. However, often scholars would stop there, as though their job had been done. But this is inadequate. The one thing we know about Kings and other historical narratives is that they were not written for the participants referred to in the narratives, but for later generations. This is what we call the rhetorical trajectory of the text. While defending the historicity of 1 and 2 Kings is important, we have to move on to ask, What is its message as a whole for later generations? Only then will we start to see that the extensive discussion in 2 Kings 17:5–41 of why the Northern and the Southern Kingdoms were taken into exile is central to the message of these two books.

As our second example, we take the delightful, small book of Jonah. When I was introduced to Jonah in seminary, front and center was a defense of its historicity. Undoubtedly this is a worthwhile discussion, but making this *the* issue prevented me for years from hearing the message of Jonah. Jonah is a masterful and suspense-filled narrative. To hear its message, you have to imagine yourself among Old Testament Israelites hearing the story told. In other words, you have to take its literary nature seriously. There are all sorts of allusions and wordplay and twists and turns that you have to pick up to hear this story in its fullness. Jonah is clearly portrayed as a prophet—but one who really does not like the idea of God being compassionate to the Assyrians, that great, brutal empire that took the Northern Kingdom into exile. As a story Jonah is disturbingly incomplete. It ends with God asking Jonah a question, and we never learn whether or not Jonah came around to God's way of thinking. This would be very unhelpful in a novel, but it is central to Jonah as kerygma, for the author is far less interested in what happened to Jonah than where we, the hearers and readers of this story, stand in relation to God's compassion to Israel's—and our—enemies.

The Bible is God-speaking literature; this is what we mean when we describe it as the Word of God. As such it teaches us a lot about God—often referred to as its propositional nature—but more than that, it invites us into a relationship with God. We will fail to hear that invitation again and again if we stop short in our work and fail to make our goal hearing God's address through his Word. We do this by attending to the kerygma of the individual books and the Bible as a whole.

Conclusion

Biblical studies can be dangerous. I suspect that there are many scholars who began studying the Bible with the motivation described in this chapter's introduction. Then they got bogged down in the historical morass that characterizes much of modern biblical studies, and soon their academic work got separated from their faith and even began to subvert it. This happens, but it need not. The way to avoid such shipwreck is to make sure that our approach to the Bible begins and builds on the foundation of the fear of the Lord. Such a hermeneutic is wonderfully liberating and calls us to explore the Bible with all the rigor we can muster, to learn from everyone we can, but all in the service of attending to God's address through it. In the process our faith will mature, and we will go on to make a major contribution toward deepening the life of God's people and blessing the world.

DISCUSSION QUESTIONS

1. Why are you doing biblical studies?
2. Have your studies thus far deepened that motivation or undermined it?
3. If the latter, has this chapter helped you to see why this has happened?
4. In this chapter I identify four "turns" in modern biblical studies. What are they, and can you explain them?
5. How should a Christian relate to mainstream, modern biblical studies?
6. In this chapter I identify three aspects of a biblical text that must be attended to if we are to hear God's address. What are they, and can you explain what they are about?
7. Use the story of the book of Jonah to explore these three aspects and their interrelationship.
8. In this chapter I argue that the most important aspect is the kerygmatic. What is this, and do you agree?

FURTHER READING

Alter, Robert, and Frank Kermode. "General Introduction." In *The Literary Guide to the Bible,* edited by Robert Alter and Frank Kermode, 1–8. London: Fontana, 1987.

Bartholomew, Craig G. *Introducing Biblical Hermeneutics: A Comprehensive Framework for Hearing God in Scripture.* Grand Rapids: Baker Academic, 2015. See especially chapters 5–7, which tell the story of the history of biblical interpretation.

———. "Post / Late? Modernity as the Context for Christian Scholarship Today." *Themelios* 22, no. 2 (January 1997): 25–38. https://biblicalstudies.org.uk/pdf /themelios/scholarship_bartholomew.pdf. This article provides an introduction to the postmodern turn.

Chrétien, Jean-Louis. *Under the Gaze of the Bible.* Translated by John Marson Dunaway. New York: Fordham University Press, 2015. See especially chapters 1–2.

"A Manifesto for Theological Interpretation." In *A Manifesto for Theological Interpretation,* edited by Craig G. Bartholomew and Heath A. Thomas, 1–25. Grand Rapids: Baker Academic, 2016.

Vanhoozer, Kevin J., et al., eds., *Dictionary for Theological Interpretation of the Bible.* Grand Rapids: Baker Academic, 2005.

DEVOTIONAL EXERCISE ─────────────────────────────────────

1. This is a challenging chapter. If your mind feels stretched, give it a break. Remember that God rules over history. Take five minutes to come to rest and silence before him.

2. Slowly read the end of Jonah several times.

   Jonah 4:9–11
   But God said to Jonah, "Is it right for you to be angry about the plant?"
   "It is," he said. "And I'm so angry I wish I were dead."
   But the LORD said, "You have been concerned about this plant, though you did not tend it or make it grow. It sprang up overnight and died overnight. And should I not have concern for the great city of Nineveh, in which there are more than a hundred and twenty thousand people who cannot tell their right hand from their left—and also many animals?"

   How do your feelings compare with those of Jonah?
   Have you ever felt really angry with God?
   What was Jonah missing in his conception of God?

3. Imagine you and Jesus sitting opposite each other in comfortable chairs. Talk to him about your feelings about God. If necessary, ask him to help you discover God's compassion.

4. We all have people who have hurt us deeply, people we might call our enemies. Name them, and then, as you are able to, hold them before God.

5. Rest in God's compassion for you, letting it encompass you.

6. Conclude your time with this prayer:

   And now may the grace of our Lord Jesus Christ, the love of God, and the fellowship of the Holy Spirit be with us all evermore.

SUGGESTED ACTIVITIES

1. Watch a film set in a premodern era with friends; for example, *The Name of the Rose*. Use this experience to think through some of the differences between the premodern era and modernity, which we discussed in this chapter.

2. Go to your library and browse through some commentaries on 1 and 2 Kings. Do you get a sense that they focus mainly on the underlying history, or do they help you access the kerygma of the text?

5

LITERATURE AND GENRE

In the previous chapter we saw that taking the literary dimension of the Bible seriously is vital to interpreting it correctly. The rediscovery of the Bible as literature in the 1970s proved very fertile for biblical interpretation in many ways. When you consult commentaries, you can see the effect of this in language such as literary structure, narrative, model reader, ideal reader, palistrophe (the ways in which one part of a text mirrors another), chiasm, inclusio, scenes and acts, plot, character development, intertextuality, and so on.

The literary turn affected not just how we read individual texts but how we understand books as a whole. In this chapter we will look at how the literary turn has revolutionized our reading of two Old Testament books, Proverbs and Psalms, then attend to its effect on our reading of the Gospels, focusing on the Gospel of Luke in particular. The Bible as literature is inseparably related to the question of genre—the type of literature we are reading—and so we will conclude by attending to the different types of genres in the Bible.

Reading Books *as* Books

Proverbs

You may have come across the "proverb a day" approach to the book of Proverbs. There is value in reading individual proverbs, but the danger lies in reading them outside their larger context. Take Proverbs 3:9–10, for example:

> Honor the LORD with your wealth,
>> with the firstfruits of all your crops;
>> then your barns will be filled to overflowing,
>> and your vats will brim over with new wine.

It is easy to see how these two verses can be read as teaching that health, wealth, and prosperity follow from honoring God. Proverbs does teach that wisdom is the way to flourishing, but Proverbs as a whole nuances this picture in important ways, recognizing that it is perfectly possible to be wise . . . and poor! In the Bible we discover the meaning of a word, a verse, a sentence, and a paragraph always in the context in which it occurs. This is a vital rule for all biblical interpretation. To use the language of Old Testament wisdom, if we do not attend to verses in context, we may interpret them foolishly rather than wisely!

In this regard an important insight in the study of Proverbs has emerged in recent decades: Proverbs as a whole has a literary shape. The prologue is 1:1–7, in which the author amasses terms to impress the reader with the value of wisdom, concluding with the great motif of Wisdom literature in 1:7 ("The fear of the LORD is the beginning of knowledge"). Proverbs 1:8–9:27 contains a series of speeches that function as the introduction to the book as a whole, setting out the ABCs of wisdom. This is done in a wonderfully creative way through the words of Lady Wisdom—wisdom personified as a woman—as well as through speeches of a father to his adolescent son. Lady Wisdom calls out in all the great public spheres of Israelite town and city life, in the law courts and the marketplace. Wisdom is rooted in a theology of creation (see 3:19–20; 8:22–31), and thus wisdom relates to all of life.

Through these speeches we learn that by far the best choice in life is to pursue wisdom; it is the path to human flourishing. The alternative is folly—the way of the fool—and it is to be avoided and rejected. Chapters 1–9 set before us this doctrine of two ways, the way of wisdom and the way of folly, and does all it can to urge us to choose wisdom (cf. Pss. 1; 2; Matt. 7:24–27).[1] For example, Proverbs 1–9 climaxes in chapter 9 with two houses, the house of Lady Wisdom and the house of Lady Folly. Both

---

1. In my view, it is likely that the two houses of Matt. 7 refer to the two houses of Prov. 9.

hostesses call to passersby to enter their house, but . . . the guests of Lady Folly are the dead (9:18)!

Proverbs 10–24 and 25–29 contain collections of what we typically think of as proverbs. These pithy sayings encapsulate wisdom as a tradition handed down among the Israelites. Not surprisingly, because of wisdom's grounding in creation, the proverbs deal with a wide diversity of topics across all of life. Many of these proverbs can be read by themselves, but it is still important to see how they relate to their contexts. We noted above how the ABCs of Proverbs 1–9 are nuanced in chapters 10–30 so that as a whole we find an educational pedagogy in Proverbs. An example of this is found in the "better . . . than" proverbs. Proverbs 28:6 is an example:

> Better the poor whose walk is blameless
> than the rich whose ways are perverse.

Whereas Proverbs 3:9–10 might make us think that the wise person will always be wealthy and prosperous, verses like Proverbs 28:6 tell us unequivocally that this is not always the case. Such verses recognize that in a fallen world sometimes the rich and wealthy will be perverse while the poor will be blameless and wise (cf. Ps. 73). The history of Israel, especially as evidenced in the Prophets, demonstrates to us that this was often the case.

The literary and kerygmatic dimensions are central to Proverbs. However, although Proverbs is not historical narrative—it is Wisdom literature— the historical dimension remains important. We see this in the book's heading (Prov. 1:1), which links Proverbs to King Solomon. As we know from 1 Kings 3–4, Solomon was particularly gifted with wisdom, so it is not surprising that much of the content of Proverbs should be associated with him. However, Proverbs itself is clear that more than one hand is at work in the book. Proverbs 25:1 refers to proverbs that were from Solomon but copied by the men (scribes) around King Hezekiah of Judah, who lived long after Solomon. Chapter 30 contains the words of Agur, and 31:1–9 has the words of King Lemuel, both unknown figures. However, Wisdom literature was not unique to Israel; in one form or another, it is found long before Israel came into existence and as a genre is pervasive across the ancient Near East. Israel shares this and many other genres with its neighbors, but Old Testament wisdom is unique in the way it is anchored in the one God, YHWH.

As a literary whole, Proverbs climaxes in the truly extraordinary description of the valiant woman in 31:11–31.[2] Fearing the Lord is the great characteristic of wisdom (see 31:30), and in chapter 31 we are given a portrait of what wisdom incarnate looks like. This section appears in a hymn (genre), a form that the book of Psalms normally reserves for God, highlighting the high praise for this woman. Like Psalm 119 discussed in chapter 1, the poem is also an acrostic poem, each section beginning with a successive letter of the Hebrew alphabet. The literary form shouts out the completeness and perfection of this woman's wisdom.

Many scholars have struggled to know why she is referred to as one who fears the Lord when none of her activities seem to be overtly religious. This misses the point and reflects a narrow view of religion. Wisdom manifests itself in all areas of life, and that is precisely what we see in Proverbs 31. The woman there is a wife and homemaker; she keeps her household well fed; she works hard; she is a businesswoman who trades in viticulture and fine fabrics; she engages in charity; and she teaches with wisdom and kindness. Her reverence for the Lord manifests itself precisely in all these areas.

Taking Proverbs seriously as literature enables us to hear its full message. Rather than offering a proverb a day, the book calls out to us as a whole, much like Lady Wisdom, urging us to seek wisdom and reject folly in all areas of life.

Psalms

As with Proverbs, it has been common to read each of the 150 psalms as separate entities. Here again the literary turn has revolutionized how we think about Psalms as a book. Certainly, it is made up of 150 psalms all recorded as Hebrew poetry, but is there more to the book than that? Recent decades of study have confirmed that there is far more.

Many factors lead us to see that the Psalter itself has a literary shape. First, it is divided into five books (Book 1, Pss. 1–41; Book 2, Pss. 42–72; Book 3, Pss. 73–89; Book 4, Pss. 90–106; Book 5, Pss. 107–150), seemingly to mirror the five books of the Pentateuch. The Pentateuch contains God's torah, his instruction for his people. The book of Psalms contains God's songs and prayers for his people as they relate to God in their effort to live

---

2. See Al Wolters, *The Song of the Valiant Woman: Studies in the Interpretation of Proverbs 31:10–31* (Carlisle, UK: Paternoster, 2001).

out his torah. Our lives need to mirror God's instruction, and here are the prayers and songs we need in order to do so.

Second, there is a clear introduction and conclusion to the Psalter. Psalms 1 and 2 are the introduction, indicated by the inclusio—the repetition of a word (or words) at the beginning and end of a section to indicate the range of the section—of "blessed" in 1:1 and 2:12. Psalm 1 focuses on the individual believer, whereas in Psalm 2 we find ourselves amid the tumult of the nations; God's torah applies to both. The Psalter concludes with Psalms 145–150, a crescendo of praise. In this way the book of Psalms as a whole moves from the blessedness of the individual believer—and nation—who delights in and meditates on YHWH's instruction to a symphony of praise of YHWH.

Third, there is a center to the Psalter. Most scholars who recognize the literary structure of Psalms find the book's center in the kingship psalms (Pss. 93–99), which celebrate YHWH as King. Indeed, if we are looking for the major theme of the Psalter, then here it is: the kingdom of God—also the central theme of Jesus's teaching in the Gospels.

A literary approach to the Psalter opens up many fresh insights and avenues for exploration.

The Gospels

The Gospels are utterly central to the Bible since they depict for us Jesus, *the* good news. The New Testament does not have one Gospel but four. On the one hand, this repetition speaks to the importance of the Christ event. On the other hand, it complicates matters, inviting careful comparison between the Gospels. The similarities between the first three led to them being called the Synoptic Gospels since they can relatively easily be seen (*optic*) together (*syn*), whereas John stands out as different and includes a great deal of material not found in the Synoptics.

The Gospels are concerned with history; they intend to tell us what happened. Our focus in this section will be on Luke's Gospel in particular, and his historical interest is clear in his prologue in Luke 1:1–4. Luke differs from the other Gospels since it is the first volume of a two-volume work, the second being Acts of the Apostles. Acts is a linchpin in the New Testament, describing as it does the explosive development of the early church after Pentecost and the spread of the gospel across the Roman Empire and beyond. Without the book of Acts, the letters of the New Testament would make no sense since they are written to churches or individuals involved in the development of the early church as presented in Acts.

Among modern interpreters, interest in history has focused on the similarities and differences between the three Synoptic Gospels. When I did graduate work in theology, a textbook we used was a Greek synopsis of the Gospels, setting the parallel texts from the three Synoptics alongside each other so that we could study them and notice, in particular, the differences between them. At that time, the sources of the Synoptics were a major area of discussion. Mark was thought to be the earliest Gospel; Matthew and Luke were thought to have used Mark as well as an additional source of the sayings of Jesus called Q. This meant that when we studied the Gospels, a great deal of energy went into examining how Luke and Matthew used Mark and the relationship between the three books. Historical issues dominated study of the Gospels, and it was difficult to move beyond this to the message of the Gospels.

Of course, there are differences between the Gospel accounts. Take the temptation of Jesus at the outset of his public ministry. Mark mentions it briefly (1:14–15). Matthew has a much longer discussion of the temptation, describing Jesus's three temptations in the following order: to turn stones into bread, to throw himself down from the pinnacle of the temple, and to worship the devil to receive the kingdoms of the world (4:1–11). Luke also has a longer discussion of the temptation, and it also refers to the three temptations, but the order of the second and third are reversed (4:1–13). John does not even refer to the temptation.

The twelve disciples were appointed by Jesus to accompany him on his public ministry and to be eyewitnesses of his life, works, and teaching. However, when he was tempted, none of them had yet been appointed and so could not and did not witness the temptation. The only way they could have known about it was through Jesus himself telling them, and this is inherently probable. However, the order in which Matthew and Luke narrate the three temptations differs. Does this matter? In my opinion, no, but it does help us see that while the Gospel writers are clear that what they tell us about happened, they are not writing history for history's sake as would contemporary historians, nor do they necessarily share historical interests that concern modern people. We might think the chronological order of the three temptations is important, but clearly for Luke and Matthew it is not. Indeed, often the Gospel writers seem to gather material together for thematic reasons and in the interests of the story they are telling rather than for strictly chronological ones.

If the Gospels are not straightforward history books, then what is their genre?[3] Clearly, they are not biographies in the modern sense of the word, although it has been argued that they do conform to the ancient Greco-Roman style of biography. What is clear is that they are historical narratives in the service of kerygma. The disciples had not only been eyewitnesses of Jesus's public ministry, but they had also witnessed his brutal death, his resurrection and ascension, and the birth of the church at Pentecost. Their lives had been transformed, and in the process they came to see that Jesus is the Messiah. It is their testimony that underlies or is present in the four Gospels.[4] In their own way, each of the four authors tells the story of Jesus in order to bear witness to him (John 21:24), so that we might receive their witness and, like them, follow Jesus. We access their messages through their narratives.

This is important not only for our reading of the Gospels but also for how we explore their historicity. The danger with the synoptic approach I describe above is that sections of different Gospels are compared apart from their literary context in a particular Gospel narrative. We need first to read each Gospel as the integrated narrative it is before we compare the books in any historical quest. This is what we will now do with Luke.

Luke 1:1–4

It is always important to take note of beginnings and endings when reading a book or passage of the Bible. With Luke's Gospel this is complex because he wrote a two-volume work. The beginning (1:1–4) is clear and fascinating.

> Many have undertaken to draw up an account of the things that have been fulfilled among us, just as they were handed down to us by those who from the first were eyewitnesses and servants of the word. With this in mind,

3. In recent years there has been considerable discussion about the genre of the Gospels. See, e.g., Francis Watson, *What Is a Gospel?* (Grand Rapids: Eerdmans, 2022). Watson argues that there are three characteristics of Gospels: they focus on the human Jesus in interaction with other humans; Jesus is the authoritative figure who mediates the divine to humans; and they are ascribed to apostles (p. 16).
4. For example, it is likely Peter's testimony underlies Mark's Gospel.

> since I myself have carefully investigated everything from the beginning, I too decided to write an orderly account for you, most excellent Theophilus, so that you may know the certainty of the things you have been taught.

We do not know exactly who Theophilus was, but he appears to have been a gentile of some standing, and his name here tells us that Luke is writing for a gentile audience. The author is Luke the physician, a companion and coworker of Paul (Col. 4:14; 2 Tim. 4:11; Philem. 1:24). The opening verses indicate Luke's awareness of other narratives about Jesus—perhaps Matthew and Mark—his connection to the original eyewitnesses of the Christ event, and his own investigations. Then Luke 1:5–2:52 plunges us into Jewish life, but these events among the Jews have universal significance.

What is not clear is where Luke's Gospel ends. Does it end in Luke 24 with the ascension and the disciples worshiping in the temple, or does it end in Acts 28 with the gospel being preached in Rome? The best answer perhaps is both, treating Luke-Acts seriously as a two-volume work.

We know from the Old Testament that the temple was a microcosm of the world for the Israelites. The boy Jesus notably refers to the temple as "my Father's house" (Luke 2:49). Interestingly, in Luke the action begins and ends in the temple (1:5–25; 24:53). Acts ends with Paul in Rome proclaiming the kingdom of God—the main theme of Jesus's teaching—and teaching about Jesus to all who would listen. The temple had begun to fulfill its universal destiny. How did that come about? Well, this is the very story Luke wants to tell Theophilus and invite him to become part of.

Luke 1:5–2:52

Luke 1:5–2:52 contains a cluster of stories relating to John the Baptist's and Jesus's births. Matthew also contains such stories, but much of this material is unique to Luke, thereby helping us see Luke's concerns in his narrative. Angels appear, the aged Elizabeth becomes pregnant with John, the virgin Mary conceives, Zechariah prophesies, Jesus is born, and a multitude of angels appears to shepherds. This is an extraordinary constellation of unusual events in a small part of Judea. And when the baby Jesus is brought to the temple, Simeon, who had been waiting for the Messiah, takes Jesus in his arms and pronounces what we now call the Nunc Dimittis (2:28–32). Similarly, the prophetess Anna thanks God and speaks to all about the redemption of Jerusalem (2:38). The events are remarkable, but it is the speeches and songs that interpret them for us. In Jesus, God's salvation has arrived, the long-awaited Messiah has come, and he will be a light for the gentiles and the glory of Israel.

Luke 2:52 is a tantalizing verse concluding this section, referring to Jesus's development and growth. From this time until the start of his public ministry we know nothing about him—some twenty years of silence (see 3:23) as he lived and developed incognito into a man. We are left wondering what Jesus will be like as the Messiah. The Jews of the day held various views of the coming Messiah. Like Mary (2:51) and those who heard about John's miraculous birth (1:66), we are left to ponder what all this will mean.

Luke 3:1–4:13

Luke 3:1–4:13 describes the emergence of Jesus in preparation for his public ministry. John the Baptist prepares his way, and Jesus comes to him to be baptized. As Jesus is praying—prayer is a distinctive and repeated theme in Luke—the heavens are opened, the Spirit descends on Jesus like a dove, and the Father pronounces, "You are my Son, whom I love; with you I am well pleased" (3:22). God is the main actor; his word comes to John (3:2), and at Jesus's baptism he affirms Jesus's association with sinners in the waters of baptism. The temptation narrative in 4:1–13 confirms what we are starting to suspect—that is, that Jesus's messiahship will not be what many were expecting or hoping for. He will eschew the route of the miraculous for his own benefit, of exotic miracles, and of the easy path to dominion over the nations. A hard path that will involve suffering lies ahead.

We noted above that Luke is writing for a gentile audience, and his genealogy of Jesus in 3:23–38 traces Jesus's ancestry back not only to King David but to Adam and to God. By comparison, Matthew, who writes primarily for Jews, shows in his genealogy that Jesus is the son of Abraham, the son of David (Matt. 1:1–17). In this way Luke foregrounds the universalism of what is happening in the Christ event and thus its relevance to gentiles. As Paul puts it, Jesus is the second Adam, and his life and death will have epochal implications for all humans, both Jew and gentile.

Luke 4:14–9:50

In Luke 4:14–9:50 we witness the start and practice of Jesus's public ministry. The so-called Nazareth Manifesto (4:16–19) sets out what Jesus's ministry will be all about: proclaiming good news to the poor, liberty to the captives, recovery of sight to the blind; freeing the oppressed; and proclaiming the year of the Jubilee. A major theme of the Gospels and of Matthew in particular is that Jesus fulfills the Old Testament (see Luke 4:21). In Luke 4:18–19, Jesus reads from Isaiah 61:1–2, clearly identifying himself as the suffering servant.[5] What is interesting is that Jesus stops short of reading the next line in Isaiah 61:2—"and the day of vengeance of our God." It is likely this omission and Jesus's references to how God worked through non-Israelites (4:23–27) that enraged the audience, which then sought to kill him. Growing opposition to Jesus and refusal to accept his interpretation of his ministry are major themes in Luke.

In chapters 4–9 we watch Jesus enact the Nazareth Manifesto, preaching and teaching, healing, calling his disciples, sending them out on a mission, and answering questions. It is a remarkable window into Jesus's ministry and thus his mission. Judea is abuzz with discussion about Jesus. Who is he? Then in 9:18–21 comes a turning point in Luke (see also Matt. 16:13–16 and Mark 8:27–29). Jesus asks his disciples who the crowds say he is. Then he personalizes the question and asks them who *they* say he is. Peter famously answers, "God's Messiah" (v. 20). In verse 21 Jesus solemnly charges them to tell no one. All sorts of false expectations were attached to the term *Messiah* among the Jews, and Jesus was not yet ready for the confrontation that would erupt when he came out publicly as the Messiah. In verse 22 he uses his favorite self-designation—"the Son of Man." As noted above, Jesus's use of this term—it is mainly found on Jesus's lips and rarely used outside of the Gospels—strongly supports the historicity of the Gospels. Daniel 7 is the real background to Jesus's use of *Son of Man*, but it was sufficiently ambiguous, unlike the term *Messiah*, that it provoked hearers to reflect on Jesus's identity without immediately engaging them in heated, vitriolic, contemporary debates.

Luke 9:51–19:48

Luke 9:51–19:48 is unique in the Synoptics in that it is structured by Jesus's long journey to Jerusalem. As Luke 9:51 says, when the time for Jesus to "be taken up" approached, he set his face to go to Jerusalem. There is

---

5. The following texts are identified by scholars as servant songs: Isa. 42:1–4; 49:1–6; 50:4–11; and 52:13–53:12. Some scholars, myself included, also see 61:1–3 as a servant song. See John N. Oswalt, *The Book of Isaiah: Chapters 40–66*, New International Commentary on the Old Testament (Grand Rapids: Eerdmans, 1998), 562–63.

a great deal of teaching in these chapters: the mission of the seventy-two (10:1–20), the parable of the good Samaritan followed by the profound Mary-Martha story (10:25–42), Jesus's teaching on prayer (11:1–13), and so on. Whether the disciples are being prepared for their mission or the crowds are being taught, everything is in the context of Jesus's resolute move toward Jerusalem. A central theme in this section is the growing opposition to Jesus and his emphasis that the Son of Man must suffer and die. In chapter 17 he cleanses lepers; in chapter 19 he makes his triumphal entry into Jerusalem and then cleanses the temple, his Father's house.

Luke 20:1–21:38

The temple features strongly in 20:1–21:38, as it did in the opening chapters of Luke. An inclusio frames the section, with both Luke 20:1 and 21:37–38 reminding us of what Jesus did in Jerusalem: he taught in the temple. The temple is God's residence among his people, and as such it is a microcosm of the world. Salvation is of the Jews, and it must issue forth from God's house. Theophilus and Jews as well as gentiles need to know this. Jesus's teaching does not go unchallenged, and the question of his authority, the state of Israel and her leaders, and warnings about what is to come are all contained in these chapters.

Luke 22:1–24:53

In chapters 22–23 the identity of Israel and Jesus is at the heart of the conflict growing around Jesus. The Passover / Last Supper is filled with this symbolism. The opposition to Jesus comes to a climax in his betrayal, arrest, and crucifixion.

The last chapter in Luke, chapter 24, tells the story of the empty tomb on the first day of the week, the remarkable Emmaus road story, and Jesus's appearance to his disciples. As on the Emmaus road, Jesus stresses how he fulfills the Old Testament and that repentance for the forgiveness of sins must be preached to all nations. While blessing his disciples, he ascends to heaven, and the disciples return from Bethany to Jerusalem, where they continually bless God in the temple. Luke's narrative—for his first volume— begins in the temple, and it ends here.

It should be clear from our discussion of Proverbs, Psalms, and Luke just how fertile approaching them as literature is. It enables us to break through many of the barriers set up by historical-critical approaches and delivers in terms of our goal of hearing their message as a whole. Now, of course, if we are going to read books as literature, we need to know what kind of literature they are. Proverbs is a wisdom book, Psalms is a hymn book, and Luke is a Gospel. As noted above the term for different types of literature is *genre*. Genre extends to whole books, as above, and to passages and individual verses. We saw, for example, just how helpful it is to know that the poem about the valiant woman in Proverbs 31 is an acrostic poem. It is thus very useful for the reader of the Bible to have a sense of the main genres in the Bible.

Genre

Letter writing may well be a lost art, with email, texting, and other forms of electronic communication having replaced it. Nevertheless, even the most ardent fans of e-communication will from time to time need to send a letter. Letters typically follow a particular form. The addresses of the recipient and the sender go at the top, the letter begins "Dear X" and ends "Yours sincerely" or "Yours faithfully," and so on. These flexible rules for letter writing in our culture are what we call genre.

Genres are culturally recognizable forms of writing, and it is important to be aware of them so that you don't make the mistake of reading a novel as a history book, instructions for a new gadget you have bought as a poem, or a legal document as a recipe that you are free to follow or not. We all have an intuitive understanding of different genres of writing; even our newest ones, like texts and tweets, have their own distinctive forms. We know, for example, that tweets can only be so many letters long, and we have grown familiar with the shorthand forms used for words in tweets and texts.

Genres emerge in cultures, and awareness of them enables us to recognize the nature of a piece of writing when we read and analyze it. There are always rules for genres, but a writer is never compelled to follow such rules slavishly. Indeed, what often makes a piece of writing most interesting is how the writer uses the genre creatively and in fresh ways. It is even possible for such creativity to forge the way for a new genre to emerge.

The biblical authors had a range of genres available to them. In the following chapters, we will attend to these in more detail. For now our aim is simply to become aware of the major genres in the Bible.

Historical Narrative

A central theme of the Bible is God's action in history, and thus, not surprisingly, large parts of the Bible are historical narrative. Genesis–Esther fits in this category, as do the four Gospels and Acts of the Apostles. As we saw above—and it is important to emphasize this point here—historical narrative in the Bible is always in the service of kerygma. The acts and speech of God are never reported merely in order to record them but in order to help the reader hear God's address today.

Law

Law was a well-known genre across the ancient Near East, Israel's cultural context. Large parts of the Pentateuch are legal literature; see, for example, Exodus 20–23 and much of Deuteronomy and Leviticus. Not surprisingly, Israel's forms are very similar to that of other ancient Near Eastern cultures—the two basic forms being casuistic and apodictic law. Casuistic law is case law and follows the form "If . . . , then . . ." An example is the laws about slavery in Exodus 21:1–11. In the text below, the repeated *ifs* and *thens* are highlighted. Note that the word *then* is not always used, but the equivalent is—namely, a consequence.

These are the laws you are to set before them:
  If you buy a Hebrew servant, he is to serve you for six years. But in the seventh year, he shall go free, without paying anything. **If** he comes alone, he is to go free alone; but **if** he has a wife when he comes, she is to go with him. **If** his master gives him a wife and she bears him sons or daughters, the woman and her children shall belong to her master, and only the man shall go free.
  But **if** the servant declares, "I love my master and my wife and children and do not want to go free," **then** his master must take him before the judges. He shall take him to the door or the doorpost and pierce his ear with an awl. **Then** he will be his servant for life.
  If a man sells his daughter as a servant, she is not to go free as male servants do. **If** she does not please the master who has selected her for himself, he must let her be redeemed. He has no right to sell her to foreigners, because he has broken faith with her. **If** he selects her for his son, he must grant her the rights of a daughter. **If** he marries another woman, he must not deprive the first one of her food, clothing and marital

rights. If he does not provide her with these three things, she is to go free, without any payment of money.

Apodictic law, by comparison, has an imperative or command form. The great example of this in the Old Testament is the Decalogue. If you read through Exodus 20:1–17 or Deuteronomy 5:1–21, you will find it full of imperatives but lacking the "If . . . , then . . ." style of casuistic law.

While Old Testament and ancient Near Eastern law is recognizable to us as law, this very recognition poses a danger. Our experience and knowledge of law have evolved over centuries, and the danger is that we impose our understanding of how law works on the Old Testament. But our understanding of law is relatively recent historically:

> When most people today think of the word "law," they have in mind what legal theorists call *statutory law*. Law, within this conception, is contained in a *codified* text. Only what is written in the code is the law. The law code supersedes all other sources of norms that preceded the formulation of the code. . . . Therefore, the courts must pay great attention to the wording of the text and cite the text in their decisions. . . . Yet as recently as the early nineteenth century the vast majority of Germans, Englishmen, and Americans thought about law in very different terms. The prevailing view for them was a *common-law* approach to jurisprudence.[6]

In common law, judges arrive at decisions on the basis of the norms and customs of a community. "Critically, the judicial decision itself does not create binding precedent. *No particular formation of these norms is final. There is no authoritative text called 'the law' or 'the law code.'* As a system of legal thought, the common law is consciously and inherently incomplete, fluid, and vague."[7]

In the ancient Near East, there was no statutory law; rather, law was of the common-law type. This has become clear through study of the ancient Near Eastern law codes we possess, such as the famous law code of the Babylonian king Hammurabi (reigned 1792–1750 BC). Scholars struggled with the fact that, despite the extensive promotion of this code evidenced by several stelae (stone slabs) and multiple manuscripts of the code, in actual legal practice Babylonian judges seem to have been under no pressure to

---

6. Joshua Berman, *Ani Maamim: Biblical Criticism, Historical Truth, and the Thirteen Principles of Faith* (Jerusalem: Maggid, 2020), 138.

7. Berman, *Ani Maamim*, 139.

follow it. The code, it seems, was a type of propaganda for Hammurabi and a resource to consider but by no means to follow slavishly.

Berman argues that Old Testament law is also common law. This is an important insight and fits well with the more accurate translation of *torah* (law) as instruction, but it needs to be nuanced carefully. Whenever we compare biblical genres with those of surrounding cultures, two criteria need to be kept in mind: the criterion of similarity and the criterion of dissimilarity. Because God reveals himself in an incarnate way, immersed in particular cultures, we rightly expect that there will be many similarities between the genres of biblical literature and those of neighboring cultures. However, because it is God who is revealing himself, we need also to pay attention to dissimilarities. This is especially true with Old Testament law.

Scholars refer to the chunks of law in the Old Testament as codes—the Covenant Code in Exodus, the Levitical Code in Leviticus, and the Deuteronomic Code in Deuteronomy—but in fact they are all embedded in historical narrative, and uniquely so in the ancient Near East. The covenant of any god with a whole people is also unique in the ancient Near East, and the blocks of law are embedded in the unfolding narrative of YHWH's immersion in the life of his people. This should give us pause, but there is something even more significant when it comes to Old Testament law. In ancient Near Eastern cultures, certain gods have a major interest in justice, but it is always the king who pronounces law. In Israel alone, however, the situation is radically different. Here YHWH is King, and he—not the Israelite king—promulgates law. This significantly alters the status of Old Testament law, a change that is confirmed by how the Old Testament itself views God's torah (see Ps. 119, for example). It does not transform Old Testament law into statutory law, but it elevates it far above being propaganda or merely a resource.

Prophecy

The ancient Near East was full of gods and their messages. The Old Testament fits well in this larger context. However, when we attend to the means of communication and the audience addressed, an important difference emerges. Priests and diviners in the ancient Near East had many ways of discerning what a god was saying, such as examining the entrails of a slaughtered animal. At festivals the statues of gods were paraded about, and their "movements" were taken to be answers to queries. Almost all of this type of divination is absent from the Old Testament. While there is some evidence in the ancient Near East for the types of prophetic speech so common in the Old Testament prophetic books—such as "Thus says the LORD . . ."—it is addressed to kings and courtiers, whereas in the Old Testament it is also addressed to all the people. This revolution in communication leads Seth Sanders to observe that we find in the Hebrew Bible / Old Testament a literature of unprecedented communicative power.[8]

YHWH, not the Israelite king, was in charge of Israel, and so not surprisingly it is especially with the rise of kingship in Israel with all its attendant dangers that we witness a parallel emergence of prophets who bring God's message to God's people, addressing king and people alike. Prophetic oracles are in a poetic form, and when we interpret them, we need to be aware of the typical forms of prophetic oracles and their nature as poetry.

Poetry

The Old Testament contains a surprising amount of poetry. In addition to the prophetic oracles, the songs of the Old Testament are in poetic form, most notably the Song of Songs and the book of Psalms. Much of the Wisdom literature (Job, Proverbs, Ecclesiastes) is also considered poetry. Job, for example, has a narrative inclusio, but the speeches of Job, his friends, and God that so dominate the book are all poetry. Proverbs 1–9 consists of poetic speeches, but the bulk of the book contains short aphoristic proverbs in poetic form.

In Hebrew poetry, as in other poetry, we find an enhanced use of metaphor, simile, assonance, and other poetic devices. We noted above, for example, how the Song of the Valiant Woman in Proverbs 31 is an acrostic poem.

However, the major characteristic of Hebrew poetry is parallelism, in which the thought expressed in one line is repeated in the next and perhaps beyond that. Repetition is absolutely central to Old Testament poetry, but scholars note that it is rarely just repetition of the thought. Generally, some intensification or development is involved. As with other poetry, readers need to develop an imaginative, literary sensibility to read the poetry of the Old Testament correctly.

Poetry is far less common in the New Testament, but it is present, most notably in passages that may be hymns or extracts of hymns from the early

---

8. Seth L. Sanders, *The Invention of Hebrew*, Traditions (Urbana: University of Illinois Press, 2009).

church. Philippians 2:6–11 is a marvelous example in this respect, and its poetic form is clear in the NIV:

> Who, being in very nature God,
>> did not consider equality with God something to be used to his
>>> own advantage;
> rather, he made himself nothing
>> by taking the very nature of a servant,
>> being made in human likeness.
> And being found in appearance as a man,
>> he humbled himself
>> by becoming obedient to death—
>>> even death on a cross!
> Therefore God exalted him to the highest place
>> and gave him the name that is above every name,
> that at the name of Jesus every knee should bow,
>> in heaven and on earth and under the earth,
> and every tongue acknowledge that Jesus Christ is Lord,
>> to the glory of God the Father.

Letters

Letters in the Old Testament are rare, but by contrast—apart from the Gospels and Acts—the New Testament consists entirely of letters. Even Revelation, a unique genre in the New Testament, begins with letters to the seven churches.

The letter form was common in the Greco-Roman world, and Paul and his fellow leaders adopted this form to communicate with the churches they planted and with one another. Letters from one party to another can present unique interpretive challenges. They often presuppose knowledge common to both parties, which an outside reader may not share. They may also be part of a chain of correspondence, but we may have only one part of the chain. This is the case with 1 and 2 Corinthians, which are likely part of a larger correspondence that some scholars have tried to reconstruct. Reading a letter is a bit like listening in on one side of a conversation, and we need to be aware of this when reading the letters of the New Testament. With some this is more the case than with others.

As we might expect, authors of New Testament letters tweaked the genre creatively in the light of the good news of Jesus. Romans and Hebrews stand out in this respect, since in both, the letter form becomes the basis for a long exposition of the Christ event, unpacked in depth and in an idiom suited to the addressees.

Conclusion

The rediscovery of the Bible as literature is an extraordinary gift, one that still has to be fully received. It should be clear from this chapter just how important it is to be attuned to the literary aspect of the Bible. We ignore it at our peril. Taken seriously, it will be a major key to rich and creative interpretation of the Bible, again and again enabling us to enter imaginatively into the world of the Bible and thereby to hear God's address.

DISCUSSION QUESTIONS

1. What do you make of the rediscovery of the Bible as literature? Does it surprise you, and if so, why?
2. Have you encountered this way of reading Proverbs, Psalms, and Luke before? In what ways do you find it helpful in listening to the Bible?
3. At the outset of this chapter, I flagged some of the many technical terms associated with the literary turn. How many of these can you remember? Revisit the introduction, make your own list, and then make sure you understand what these terms mean. Use a dictionary or online resource as needed.
4. What does *genre* mean, and why is it so important for biblical interpretation?
5. How would you categorize the genre of the following books?
   - John
   - 1 and 2 Kings
   - Psalms
   - 1 Corinthians
   - Job
6. Parallelism is a dominant characteristic of Hebrew / Old Testament poetry. Choose any psalm, and see if you can identify the parallelism in some of its verses.

FURTHER READING

Bartholomew, Craig G. *Introducing Biblical Hermeneutics: A Comprehensive Framework for Hearing God in Scripture*. Grand Rapids: Baker Academic, 2015. See especially chapter 11, "Literature."

———. *Reading Proverbs with Integrity*. Cambridge: Grove, 2001.

Bartholomew, Craig G., and Andrew West, eds. *Praying by the Book: Reading the Psalms*. Carlisle, UK: Paternoster, 2002.

Green, Joel B. "Learning Theological Interpretation from Luke." In *Reading Luke: Interpretation, Reflection, Formation*, edited by Craig G. Bartholomew, Joel B. Green, and Anthony C. Thiselton, 55–78. Scripture and Hermeneutics Series 6. Grand Rapids: Zondervan Academic, 2005.

McCann, J. Clinton, Jr. *A Theological Introduction to the Book of Psalms: The Psalms as Torah*. Nashville: Abingdon, 1993.

Osborne, Grant R. *The Hermeneutical Spiral: A Comprehensive Introduction to Biblical Interpretation*. 2nd ed. Downers Grove, IL: IVP Academic, 2006. See especially part 2. Osborne has a major focus on genre.

DEVOTIONAL EXERCISE

1. Savoring literature takes leisurely time. So does our relationship with God. Take five minutes to slow down and come to stillness in God's presence.

2. Your story is part of the Bible's grand story. Reflect on this amazing truth, and respond to God accordingly.

3. Read the following passage slowly several times.

   Psalm 1
   Blessed is the one
       who does not walk in step with the wicked
   or stand in the way that sinners take
       or sit in the company of mockers,
   but whose delight is in the law of the LORD,
       and who meditates on his law day and night.
   That person is like a tree planted by streams of water,
       which yields its fruit in season

and whose leaf does not wither—
    whatever they do prospers.
Not so the wicked!
    They are like chaff
    that the wind blows away.
Therefore the wicked will not stand in the judgment,
    nor sinners in the assembly of the righteous.
For the LORD watches over the way of the righteous,
    but the way of the wicked leads to destruction.

Psalm 2
Why do the nations conspire
    and the peoples plot in vain?
The kings of the earth rise up
    and the rulers band together
    against the LORD and against his anointed, saying,
"Let us break their chains
    and throw off their shackles."
The One enthroned in heaven laughs;
    the Lord scoffs at them.
He rebukes them in his anger
    and terrifies them in his wrath, saying,
"I have installed my king
    on Zion, my holy mountain."
I will proclaim the LORD's decree:
He said to me, "You are my son;
    today I have become your father.
Ask me,
    and I will make the nations your inheritance,
    the ends of the earth your possession.
You will break them with a rod of iron;
    you will dash them to pieces like pottery."
Therefore, you kings, be wise;
    be warned, you rulers of the earth.
Serve the LORD with fear
    and celebrate his rule with trembling.
Kiss his son, or he will be angry
    and your way will lead to your destruction,
for his wrath can flare up in a moment.
    Blessed are all who take refuge in him.

Does the NIV heading "Book 1" mean more to you now than it did before?

What do you learn about the blessedness of the individual (Ps. 1) and of nations (Ps. 2)?

Reflect on your own experience of blessedness.

Are there ways you can increase this experience?

The blessed person meditates on God's instruction (Ps. 1:2). Pick one verse that stands out to you and do that now for five minutes.

4. Imagine Jesus sitting opposite you and discuss with him your desire to be blessed.

5. Conclude your time with this prayer:

> And now may the grace of our Lord Jesus Christ, the love of God, and the fellowship of the Holy Spirit be with us all, evermore. Amen.

SUGGESTED ACTIVITIES

Even as we attend to the Bible as literature, it is important to remember that many of the original hearers would have heard the Bible read out loud to them. Indeed, some of the literary techniques in biblical texts are designed to make memorization easier.

1. Choose a short psalm and study it closely, perhaps using a good commentary like James L. Mays, *Psalms*, Interpretation: A Bible Commentary for Teaching and Preaching (Louisville: Westminster John Knox, 1994).

2. Having studied the psalm, find someone who can teach you to chant it, as some Anglicans and Catholics do. Use the chanting of the psalm to memorize it, so that it becomes a pacemaker in your consciousness.

3. Reflect on ways in which this experience has helped you better to understand the psalm and to carry it into your life.

6

NARRATIVE AND HISTORY

Many people know that the church in Corinth was beset with problems. What is not as well known is that one of their problems was that they denied the historicity of a major event in Jesus's life—namely, the resurrection.

In 1 Corinthians 15:1–11 Paul provides a beautiful and succinct review of the gospel. Verses 4–5 sum up his message: it is all about Jesus Christ who died for our sins, was buried, was raised, and appeared to the disciples, all in accordance with the Scriptures (the Old Testament). However, as we see from verses 12–19, some in Corinth denied the resurrection of the dead. Paul says if they are correct, then Christ could not have been raised from the dead. This is catastrophic for the Christian faith: "And if Christ has not been raised, our preaching is useless and so is your faith" (v. 14).

Why History Matters

Why is it so important that Christ actually rose from the dead? Isn't it just as good if we find the story of his resurrection helpful even if it didn't happen, or if he has risen in our hearts even if his body remained in the tomb? Not according to Paul and the Bible. How language works can help us here.

The lecture notes of Oxford philosopher John L. Austin (1911–1960) were published as *How to Do Things with Words*. He taught at a time when it was commonly argued that only statements or propositions made sense and were thus logically and scientifically respectable. Austin affirmed the importance of propositions but argued that there was another type of language that was as important—namely, performative language. If one thing we do with language is to make statements, then there are also a whole lot of other, equally meaningful things that we do with language—that is, perform actions. For example, by means of language we can issue a warning, encourage someone, pronounce a man and a woman husband and wife, baptize a person, and so on. Through language we actually perform such actions. A famous example of Austin's is that of the Queen standing next to a ship and breaking a bottle of champagne over its bough and pronouncing it the *Queen Mary*. Through her speech the Queen performed the action of christening the ship.

Austin's view of language has come to be known as speech act theory. It is a theory of how we act by means of and through speech. Austin developed his theory about how language works by identifying three parts of a speech act: the locution, the illocution, and the perlocution. This may be complex language, but it's easily understood. The locution refers to the basic meaning of a sentence, a sentence that makes sense. Consider the following sentence: There is a snake in the garden. None of us have any difficulty making sense of this sentence. We know what a snake is, we know what a garden is, and the grammar of the sentence works. This would not be the case if we came across the following: a garden snake a in is There.

So far so good, the locution is clear. But think about the sentence above. What might a speaker be doing with this sentence? What is the force of the sentence? It could, for example, be a warning, alerting the hearer to a dangerous snake in the garden and the need to be careful. For lovers of snakes, it could be an invitation to come and see. Or "snake" could be used here as a metaphor for a particularly vicious person, and the speaker is drawing the attention of the person he is addressing to their presence in the garden. Yet again, both "snake" and "garden" could be used metaphorically to let the hearer know there is a dangerous person or thing at work in a situation.

The context of a sentence alone will make clear the force of the statement. Austin calls the force of a statement its illocution. If the sentence above intends to warn about the presence of a dangerous snake, then the illocutionary force of the sentence is that of a warning.

Finally, the perlocution of a statement is its effect on the hearer. If, like me, you are wary of snakes, then the effect of the warning would be that you avoid the garden.

A further element in Austin's theory is that for a speech act to work, certain conditions have to be met. For example, for the sentence above to be a warning about a snake in the garden, there actually has to be a snake in the garden. For the *Queen Mary* to have actually been christened, it must be the Queen herself standing there and breaking the bottle over the bough of the ship. For a couple to actually be married when the words "I now pronounce you man and wife" are spoken, the speaker needs to be a minister with such powers. If one of us dresses up as royalty, goes down to the harbor, and breaks a bottle of champagne over the bough of a ship, saying, "I now pronounce you the *King Alfred*," the speech act, according to Austin, misfires and is invalid.

How does this help us with the historicity of the resurrection? In brief, speech act theory helps us to see that if the resurrection never happened, then Paul's message and that of the entire New Testament misfires; it is rendered invalid.

A Network of Beliefs

Of course, we could still ask, Was Paul right? Does the Christian faith really depend on the great acts of God recorded in the Bible, like the resurrection, actually having taken place? Theologians refer to such events as special divine action.

In order to answer this question, we have to reflect on the Bible's view of God and the world. The basic distinction in the Bible is between the uncreated God and the created world. God transcends the world but is also immanently involved in it. Another way of stating this is to say that the Bible does not provide us with a deistic view of God. According to deism, God set up the world and then left it to itself, a bit like winding up an alarm clock and then leaving it to unwind. The Bible affirms that God sets up the world but, unlike deism, insists that he remains deeply involved with it.

The word we use for God's relationship to the world is *providence*. There are three aspects to God's providence. First, God sustains the world in existence; second, he accompanies it on its journey through time; and third, he rules over it, leading it to the destination he intends for it. All three of these aspects of providence speak deeply to God's profound engagement with his world, the world that he ushered into existence. To use the language of Genesis 1–3, God speaks by divine command the diversified world into existence; he sees the world as it diversifies and pronounces it good and very good; he addresses Adam and Eve; he walks with Adam in the great park of Eden; he comes looking for Adam after the fall; and he pronounces judgment on the first couple and the serpent. Genesis 1–3 is replete with language of divine action. God is God, but he is not far off; he speaks to his image bearers and is actively engaged in his world.

From this perspective, while God's action cannot be limited to special divine action, we would certainly expect God to speak and to intervene and act in the world. Not to expect this is to fall into deism. The witness of the whole Bible is that this is indeed what God does, and the narrative of the Bible shows us many different ways in which God acts at key moments. Of these, two examples soar above the others in the Bible: the exodus-Sinai event in the Old Testament, and the Christ event in the New Testament. Creation is, of course, the indispensable background and context for both of these. In the Old Testament all paths lead to and away from Sinai. According to the New Testament, Jesus is the second Moses (Matt. 5–7) and one far superior to Moses (Heb. 3:1–6); for Christians the Christ event surpasses all other events as good news.

Thus, to deny God's action in history is to take a very different view of God and the world from that presented by the Bible. This makes the historicity of God's actions vitally important. There is a great deal at stake in the fact that the exodus and the Sinai event took place, that Christ did become incarnate and tabernacle among us, and so on.

This raises the crucial question of how we can be sure such events happened. Situating them within their indispensable network of beliefs is illuminating in this respect. We noted above that the doctrine of creation is the crucial backdrop for divine action, so we can ask, for example, How can we be sure the world is God's creation? Hebrews 11:3 answers this question as follows: "By faith we understand that the universe was formed at God's command, so that what is seen was not made out of what was visible."

There are undoubtedly very good reasons for believing that the world is God's good creation, and such reasons are important for apologetics and to buttress our faith, but Hebrews is right that ultimately it is through faith that we come to this understanding. Conversion brings with it a worldview. At the heart of this worldview is the trinitarian God who has come to us in

Jesus, and when we enter a personal relationship with Jesus, trust in the Bible as God's Word follows, as does a view of this world and ourselves as God's creation. Faith carries with it the assurance that God has acted in Jesus to secure our redemption and that of the whole creation.

If this sounds circular, it is! Ultimately, our worldview or orientation toward the world is grounded in faith, whether we are a Christian or not. The Spirit brings us assurance that this is the true view of the world, assuring us of God's existence and trinitarian nature, of the world as creation, and of God's acts in the world. To make certainty about such truths dependent on us would put us, rather than God, in the driver's seat, thereby turning the world of the Bible upside down.

Fortunately, you do not need to take just my word for it. In recent decades there has been a remarkable renaissance of Christian philosophy. The distinguished Christian philosopher Alvin Plantinga precisely addresses the issues we are discussing.[1] Plantinga and a number of other Christian philosophers have argued rigorously that belief in God is properly basic. What they mean by this is that belief in God is arrived at by faith through the work of the Spirit and is warranted (rationally justified) to be held apart from reasons for it. This does not mean that there are not good reasons for such belief—there are—but that our belief in God does not ultimately depend on such reasons. This is good news. As you may well have experienced, if your belief in God depends on arguments and apologetics, then it will easily become like a house of cards, susceptible to shifting arguments.

Belief in the trinitarian God carries with it other beliefs as noted above, including beliefs about the Bible as the Word of God. In his chapter "Defeaters? Historical Biblical Criticism," Plantinga distinguishes between traditional biblical commentary and historical biblical criticism (HBC). Three features characterize the former:

- Scripture is an infallible guide to morals and faith since it is God's revelation to us.
- The primary author of the whole Bible is God.
- One can't always determine the meaning of a biblical passage by what the human author had in mind.

1. For Alvin Plantinga's accessible account, see his *Knowledge and Christian Belief* (Grand Rapids: Eerdmans, 2015), esp. chap. 8 on historical criticism. For his more detailed account, see his *Warranted Christian Belief* (New York: Oxford University Press, 2000).

HBC is an Enlightenment project and seeks to investigate the Bible on the basis of reason alone, apart from faith. Plantinga discerns two types of HBC: Troeltschian HBC—named after Ernst Troeltsch (1865–1923), a German, liberal Protestant theologian—which excludes the very possibility of divine action in its analysis, and Duhemian HBC—named after the French physicist Pierre Duhem (1861–1916)—which seeks to study the Bible apart from any metaphysical or religious presuppositions but without excluding the possibility of divine action. He notes:

> Thus the Duhemian scriptural scholar wouldn't take for granted either that God is the principal author of the Bible or that the main lines of the Christian story are in fact true; these are not accepted by all who are party to the discussion. She wouldn't take for granted that Jesus rose from the dead, or that any other miracle has occurred; she couldn't so much as take it for granted that miracles are possible (because their possibility is rejected by many who are party to the discussion). On the other hand, of course, Duhemian scriptural scholarship can't take it for granted that Christ did not rise from the dead or that no miracles have occurred, or that miracles are impossible.[2]

For the Duhemian approach, accepting the resurrection of Jesus requires more evidence, as well as agreement among scholars.

Plantinga recognizes that there is a great deal to be learned from HBC. However, he correctly sees that the epistemology—how we come to true knowledge—informing HBC of both types is very different from that entailed in a Christian view of the world. He concludes that "the traditional Christian can rest easy with the claims of HBC; she need feel no obligation, intellectual or otherwise, to modify her belief in the light of its claims and alleged results."[3]

Far from this making us uninterested in history and the Bible, it should make us all the more interested. As Christians we have every reason to be interested in the historical aspect of the Bible, and we should be deeply concerned to explore the complex issues that emerge in this area.

Narrative and History

As we noted in chapter 5, large parts of the Bible are historical narrative. The literary form in which God's actions in the world are relayed to us is

---

2. Plantinga, *Knowledge and Christian Belief*, 101.
3. Plantinga, *Knowledge and Christian Belief*, 106.

narrative. A synonym for narrative is *story*, and we may wonder if such a characterization does not already raise questions about the historicity of the history books of the Bible. If history is about "what happened," do not the very words *narrative* or *story* detract from the historicity of the Bible? Several points need to be noted in this respect.

First, we need to distinguish between history and historiography, the writing of history. If we generally define *history* as what happened in the past, then it will be immediately clear that historiography can never contain all that happened. Every day millions and millions of things happen in the world, and thus it is inevitable that historians will be *selective* in what they focus on in the attempt to tell the story of what happened. It is impossible for this not to be the case, and once we understand this, the historian's criteria for selection become most interesting. For example, Marxist historians focus in particular on the role of economics in history, and they inevitably drill down on economic causes in the way they narrate history. Other historians will look at similar periods of history but tell their stories differently.

Second, historians inevitably use narrative as they seek not just to expose historical facts but to show how they are connected to one another. All history writers base their work on hard evidence, but they seek to construct a narrative of what they are studying. This narrative does not just emerge with the evidence; historians never just hold up a mirror to the past. From the available evidence they construct a narrative, and to an important extent the final result is a combination of the evidence and what they bring to it.

Third, since both history writing and fiction use narrative, how can we tell the difference between them? Before we address this, it is important to remember that fiction can be true. Some scholars argue that parts of the Bible can only be true if the events described in them actually happened. Unlike history writing, fiction never claims to be an accurate representation of the past, but in its own way it can be as true. The parables of Jesus are a great example of this. No one doubts that they are fictional, but this does not for a moment make them untrue.

Can the literary forms or poetics of fiction and those of historical narrative help us distinguish the two from each other? It is easy to slip into the belief that they can. Let me give a personal example. I do think that Job is probably fiction, but for a long time one of my reasons for this view was simply wrong. The endless speeches of Job's friends are all Hebrew poetry, and I assumed that they therefore could not be historical. However, this is simply wrong. Another example is the argument by some scholars that since much of the material in Exodus may be from Israel's liturgy, it cannot be historical. Again this is simply wrong. As detailed studies by the philosopher Paul Ricoeur and work on the Hebrew Bible (the Old Testament) by Meir Sternberg and others have shown, the poetics at work in fiction and historical narrative can be the same. Poetic form can be and is used to tell about what actually happened. The exodus is an example. In the book of Exodus, the narration of this triumphal event is told by the Israelites in song, a poetic form (Exod. 15:1–18), perhaps composed by Miriam (Exod. 15:20–21). The song is preceded by the narrative of the events of the exodus, confirming that the story of what actually took place can be reported in prose *and* in poetry. The form in which the story of the exodus is told does not tell us whether the events described are fictional or historical. If Job is fictional, it is not because the speeches are in poetry.

How then do we distinguish between fiction and historiography? We do this by means of the intention of the author(s). As Baruch Halpern observes, "Whether a text is history, then, depends on what its author meant to do."[4] If this is correct, then the question of authorial intentions of historical narratives in the Bible arises. However, biblical authors rarely state their intentions—with exceptions being Luke (1:1–4) and John (20:30–31; 21:24–25)—so in most cases we have to determine the intention from the text. Such determination is linked back into the network of beliefs we spoke about above, and so Meir Sternberg is right when he says of the Hebrew Bible / Old Testament, "The product is neither fiction nor historicized fiction nor fictionalized history, but historiography pure and uncompromising."[5] For Sternberg all the evidence points in this direction: Israel's obsession with remembering the past—not least because of its relevance in the present—and the uniqueness of Israel in this regard among the nations of the ancient Near East. "Were the narrative written or read as fiction, then God would turn from the lord of history into a creature of the imagination, with the most disastrous results."[6]

4. Baruch Halpern, *The First Historians: The Hebrew Bible and History* (San Francisco: Harper & Row, 1988), 8.
5. Meir Sternberg, *The Poetics of Biblical Narrative: Ideological Literature and the Drama of Reading* (Bloomington: Indiana University Press, 1985), 35.
6. Sternberg, *Poetics of Biblical Narrative*, 32.

However, fourth, we need to recognize that none of the historical narratives in the Bible were written simply as a record of "what happened." This is the danger with Sternberg's comment above that the Old Testament is "historiography pure and uncompromising." A disinterested view of history writing, as we have grown to expect, is foreign to the Bible. In chapter 4 we introduced the threefold cord of interpretation: historical, literary, and theological. The theological element, which we will come to in the next chapter, is the kerygma of the text. This is not just one of the three but the dominant one. In the biblical books, literature and history are all in the service of kerygma. John 21:24 speaks of the disciple who authored John's Gospel as the one who testifies concerning these things. The verb for "testify" is *martyreō*, from which we get our English word *martyr*, a reminder that this is not neutral testimony but testimony designed to bring us to faith in Jesus (cf. John 20:30–31). As we will see in the next chapter, the dominance of kerygma is a vital clue for listening to the Bible.

Finally, we need to be careful of projecting contemporary ways of writing history back onto the Bible. There is no doubt that the Israelites and the authors of the Bible were well able to distinguish between something that happened and something that did not happen. Indeed, flowing out of their encounter with and worship of YHWH, the Israelites developed a novel view of history and its importance, which we continue to benefit from today. Herbert Butterfield (1900–1979), one of the major historians of the twentieth century and a Protestant Christian, was Regius Professor of History and Vice Chancellor of the University of Cambridge. In *The Origins of History*, he has a remarkable chapter entitled "The Originality of the Hebrew Scriptures." Having reviewed the ancient Near East in the chapters leading up to this one, he observes, "Then, suddenly, one finds oneself confronted with what must be the greatest surprise in the whole story. There emerges a people not only supremely conscious of the past but possibly more obsessed with history than any other nation that has ever existed. The very key to its whole development seems to have been the power of its historical memory. . . . Everything hung on men's attachment to a single event that could never be forgotten."[7] This nation is ancient Israel.

There is indeed something radically new and unique about the way in which history functions in the Old Testament. Nevertheless, the Israelites

7. Herbert Butterfield, *The Origins of History* (New York: Basic Books, 1981), 80–81.

were an ancient Near Eastern people, and we need to determine their approach to history writing inductively from the texts of the Old Testament and in comparison with the history writing of other nations. For example, it might seem to us that if the Ten Commandments are repeated, they must be repeated word for word, as is evident in so many churches in which they adorn the walls. However, the authors of Exodus 20 and Deuteronomy 5 clearly felt no such compulsion. In both chapters we clearly find the Ten Commandments, but as is often noted, there are many minor differences between them. This may seem to be a problem for us; clearly it was not one for the authors of the Old Testament.

The Example of Exodus 19–24: God at Sinai

We noted above the importance of Sinai in the Old Testament. Everything in the Old Testament leads to Sinai and all roads lead away from it. Doubtless you are familiar with the narrative. YHWH rescues his people from brutal slavery and oppression in Egypt and then leads them to Sinai, where he meets with them and establishes a legal, covenant relationship with them. At the heart of this covenant in Exodus 20 is the Ten Commandments.

When historical narrative is dealing with something that is very important, it invariably slows down. This is true, for example, in the Gospels. Martin Kähler describes Mark's Gospel as a "passion narrative with an extended introduction."[8] Whether this is fair or not, it helpfully reminds us of the importance placed by the Gospel writers upon the arrest, crucifixion, and resurrection of Jesus. Their stories slow down at this point, signaling the importance of what is being recounted.

This is certainly true of Sinai. We will focus in this section on Exodus 19–24, but it is important to realize that Israel remains at Sinai from Exodus 19, when they arrive there, through Numbers 10:11–13, when they depart from Sinai. This is a large part of the Pentateuch, and the slowing of the narrative is particularly evident in the account of God's commanding the Israelites to build his royal house—the tabernacle—and their building of it. The detailed instructions and then the detailed account of how the instructions were obeyed strike the modern reader as tedious and perhaps unnecessarily prolonged. However, the lengthy repetition indicates the

---

8. Martin Kähler, *The So-Called Historical Jesus and the Historic, Biblical Christ*, trans. Carl E. Braaten (Minneapolis: Fortress, 1964), 80n11.

enormity of what is going on. God is setting up his house among the Israelites, and he will dwell among them from now on. This is a kind of Eden regained, and it is wonderfully important.

God's dwelling among his people is a result of the covenant between God and his people, the covenant that is validated in Exodus 24. The actual ritual formalizing the covenant is in verses 3–8. It is preceded by God's command that Moses, Aaron, Nadab, Abihu, and the seventy elders of Israel come up the mountain to YHWH, and it is followed by the narrative of their doing so. We will return to the question of the actual chronology below, but the theology and kerygma of this text become clear when we see what those who went up the mountain experienced. Extraordinarily, they saw God, were not harmed, and enjoyed a meal (24:9–11)! The meal is a remarkable sign of the communion now shared between the Israelites and God. The seventy elders represent the whole of Israel—with possible evocations of the nations of the world, seventy of which are listed in the Table of the Nations in Genesis 10. In his Old Testament theology, Vriezen argues that communion is at the heart of the Old Testament—indeed, of the whole Bible: "This certainty of the immediate communion between the Holy God and weak, sinful man may be called the underlying idea of the whole of the Biblical testimony, for in essence this basic idea is also found in the New Testament."[9] We will return to this theme in the next chapter.

Exodus 24 is instructive in other ways for our discussion. As noted above, in verses 1–2 YHWH instructs Moses to ascend the mountain with this group. However, in verses 3–8 Moses performs the ceremony ratifying the covenant. It is only in verse 9 that God's instruction to Moses is carried out. What is going on with this strange order of events? We would expect verses 1–2 to be followed immediately by verses 9–18. Such a strange ordering of events—to us—is not unusual in the Old Testament and is an example of resumptive repetition. Brichto has done definitive work on this literary trope, and he defines it as follows:

> Essentially it is the treatment of one event two times. The first narration of the event . . . is usually briefer . . . than the second [and] is an independent, freestanding literary unit. The second treatment or episode, usually longer than the first, may or may not be able to stand by

9. Th. C. Vriezen, *An Outline of Old Testament Theology*, 2nd ed. (Oxford: Blackwell, 1970), 157. Cf. John 17:3.

itself. . . . The second treatment seems to go back to the opening point of the first episode and, resuming the theme of that treatment, provide a more detailed account . . . of how the bottom line of the first episode . . . was arrived at. . . . The variety and richness of effects made possible by this technique are such that a full appreciation can only be achieved by examining each instance in situ.[10]

It will be apparent just how this fits with Exodus 24. Verses 9–18 could stand by themselves, but clearly they resume what is begun in verses 1–2. This is a good example of resumptive repetition, though the repetition makes working out the chronology of what happened challenging. The logic of the passage's arrangement would appear to be as follows: Knowing what we do about the boundaries of holiness around the mountain from chapter 19, it comes as a shocking surprise that such a group is invited up the mountain. How is this possible in the light of the strong warnings in chapter 19? The answer is the ratification of the covenant in verses 3–8. The covenant changes the way the boundaries operate so that representatives of all the Israelites can ascend the mountain, see God, and enjoy a meal in his presence. In this way the repetition makes important theological points while leaving the precise chronology unclear. Clearly the ratification of the covenant takes place before the group ascends the mountain, but does God give his instructions before the ceremony? That remains unclear.

Historical critics regard Exodus 19–24 as a deeply problematic text, especially in terms of its literary unity. For example, Ska observes that "the Sinai pericope is one of the most complicated passages in the entire Pentateuch."[11] The sort of data that historical critics refer to and find confusing are the repeated references to Moses ascending and descending the mountain.[12] We have already seen how resumptive repetition helps make sense of Exodus 24, and Sprinkle argues that it helps account for many of the surface difficulties that historical critics discern in chapters 19–24.[13]

---

10. Herbert C. Brichto, *Toward a Grammar of Biblical Poetics: Tales of the Prophets* (New York: Oxford University Press, 1992), 13–14. For resumptive repetition and Exod. 19–24, see Craig G. Bartholomew, *The God Who Acts in History: The Significance of Sinai* (Grand Rapids: Eerdmans, 2020).

11. Jean-Louis Ska, *Introduction to Reading the Pentateuch*, trans. Sr. Pascale Dominique (Winona Lake, IN: Eisenbrauns, 2006), 213.

12. See Exod. 19:3, 7, 8, 14, 20, 21; 24:1, 9, 12, 18; 32:7, 15.

13. Joe M. Sprinkle, *"The Book of the Covenant": A Literary Approach*, Journal for the Study of the Old Testament Supplement Series 174 (Sheffield: Sheffield Academic Press, 1994).

Sprinkle argues that Exodus 19:16–25 is a synopsis of the theophany at Sinai as a whole, and the sections that follow—namely, the Ten Commandments (20:1–17), the terror of the Israelites (20:17–21), and the laws (20:22–23:33)—all take place simultaneously with 19:16–25. Exodus 24:1–2 is itself a resumption of Exodus 19:24. According to Sprinkle, Exodus 20:18 contains a circumstantial clause with a participle in order to flag resumptive repetition, reverting back to Exodus 19:16–19. Thus, Exodus 20:21 is not another ascent by Moses but the same one mentioned in 19:20. For Sprinkle the Ten Commandments themselves are a repetition and should be located somewhere in the events of 19:18–20. This repetition of ascents (19:20; 20:21) means that the laws of this section were given to Moses after his ascent in 19:20 but before his descent in 19:25. Sprinkle argues that the laws of 20:22–23:33 expand upon the Ten Commandments.

If this is correct, then it goes a long way toward resolving the tensions that historical critics discern in chapters 19–24. However, we may well ask why the author would arrange his material in this way. Sprinkle suggests five reasons:

- As a literary technique, resumptive repetition allows for an elaboration of actions taking place at the same time.
- A nonchronological arrangement like this allows for materials such as the Ten Commandments to be set apart for didactic purposes. Placing the terror of the people after the Ten Commandments presents the fear of YHWH as the proper response to the theophany.
- Resumptive repetition enables different perspectives to be presented, such as that of YHWH versus that of the people.
- Sprinkle argues that we find in 19–24 a pattern of narrative-law-narrative that is set out chiastically—that is, an arrangement in which elements mirror each other, as represented below.

A Narrative: the covenant offered (19:3–25)

   B Laws (general): the Ten Commandments (20:1–17)

      C Narrative: the terror of the people (20:18–21)

   B′ Laws (specific): the Book of the Covenant (20:22–23:33)

A′ Narrative: the covenant ratified (24:1–11)

For Sprinkle the implication of this structure is that the emphasis is on A—namely the giving and receiving of the covenant—with C pointing to the appropriate response: the fear of YHWH.

Where does this leave us in terms of the chronology of what happened at Sinai? First, we should note that a text like Exodus 19–24 is performing multiple actions or illocutions, to return to speech act theory, at the same time. There is nothing unusual about this. Simultaneously the text is telling the reader what happened and instructing the reader—its didactic purpose. We should remember that most Israelites would hear and receive this text orally, as it was taught to them by the priests. Thus, it is doubtless written so that it could be heard and memorized easily.

Second, we should note that an effect of the text's literary arrangement is that it is not easy to reconstruct the chronology with the sort of precision we might desire. On the basis of his analysis, Sprinkle discerns the following order of events:

- The narrative begins in chapter 19 with the Israelites' arrival at Sinai and with Moses bringing them to the mountain where the theophany takes place.
- Moses calls to God, and God answers him in thunder, or so it seems to the Israelites. The thunder includes God speaking at least part of the Ten Commandments.
- The Israelites are terrified, and Moses tries to reassure them. He ascends the mountain where he receives the remainder of the Ten Commandments and the explanatory laws.
- At God's instruction Moses descends to remind the Israelites not to transgress the boundaries of the mountain, and then he ascends again with Aaron and the others.
- The ratification of the covenant takes place before Moses and the others ascend.

Exodus 19–24 is a complex text, and we are indebted to historical critics for their rigorous analysis of its details. The literary approach outlined above reminds us that the same data historical critics analyze is capable of more than one interpretation. In philosophy of science, no less, this is what is referred to as theory being underdetermined by the facts. In other words, historical critics helpfully foreground the data, such as Moses ascending and descending, but there is more than one way of accounting for this. The historical critics' way is to see the data as reflecting various sources that have been poorly stitched together; these sources can then be reconstructed. Sprinkle's type of reading takes the same data but allows us to see how chapters 19–24 can be read as a literary unity. Ockham's razor—the simplest explanation is probably the right one—favors Sprinkle's approach.

Does all this matter? Indeed it does. At the heart of the Sinai theophany are the Ten Commandments. These are central to the whole Bible and to Christian ethics in general. Note how they are prefaced in Exodus 20:1–2. Verse 1 tells us they are spoken by God. This is an example of special divine action, and the commandments' authority rests on their origin in God himself. Verse 2 informs us that the one speaking is YHWH, the name of God especially associated with the rescue of the Israelites from harsh slavery in Egypt (see Exod. 3 and 6). In verse 2 we learn that the commandments are premised on YHWH's action of bringing the Israelites out of Egypt. To refer to speech act theory again, the commandments would misfire if YHWH had not in fact rescued the Israelites from Egypt and brought them to himself at Sinai, where and in which context he spoke these words.

Sinai, as noted, is absolutely central to the Old Testament. And central to it is divine action in history. There is thus a great deal at stake in working out how historical reference—what actually happened—and the literary shape of the narrative are woven together. Anyone who has done mainstream Old Testament studies knows all too well that one problem with historical-critical readings of Exodus 19–24 is that, having determined that the chapters are fragmented and unreadable as is, most energy then goes into speculative reconstruction of the sources that are thought to underlie the text. Doubtless the author(s) used sources, but we do not have these; any such reconstruction is speculative and uncertain. More than that, this approach creates a barrier to discerning the most important aspect of Exodus 19–24—that is, its kerygma. It is to kerygma that we turn in the next chapter.

DISCUSSION QUESTIONS

1. Is "what happened in the past" an adequate definition of *history*? Explain.

2. Why does it matter that Jesus actually rose from the dead?

3. What is speech act theory and how does it help us with the question above?

4. On what main basis do you believe that Jesus rose from the dead?

5. Can fiction be true? Explain and provide examples.

6. The many long chapters of speeches in Job are all in poetry. Does this mean that the book is not historical? Explain.

7. As Christians why should we take God's action in history seriously?

FURTHER READING

Evans, C. Stephen. *The Historical Christ and the Jesus of Faith: The Incarnational Narrative as History*. Oxford: Clarendon, 1996.

Herberg, Will. "Biblical Faith as 'Heilsgeschichte' [Salvation History]: The Meaning of Redemptive History in Human Existence." In *Faith Enacted as History: Essays in Biblical Theology*, edited by Bernhard W. Anderson, 32–42. Philadelphia: Westminster, 1976.

Plantinga, Alvin. *Knowledge and Christian Belief*. Grand Rapids: Eerdmans, 2015. See especially chapter 8.

Robinson, Marilynne. "Moses." *Salmagundi* 121/122 (Winter–Spring 1999), https://salmagundi.skidmore.edu/articles/13-moses. A common criticism of the Bible is not so much that it is unhistorical but that it is immoral. The well-known novelist and essayist Marilynne Robinson weighs in on that debate with respect to Moses in this article.

Wright, N. T. *The New Testament and the People of God*. Minneapolis: Fortress, 1992. See especially chapter 4. This volume is part of an entire series worth reading, Wright's magisterial Christian Origins and the Question of God.

DEVOTIONAL EXERCISE

1. History is his story. Amid all that is going on in the world, rest in this truth, and take five minutes to come to silence before God.

2. God is deeply involved in his world and in your life. Reflect on the encouragement and mystery of this. Take several minutes to be open to God amid all life's mysteries.

3. Read the following passage several times and reflect on it.

> **Mark 1:40–44**
>
> A man with leprosy came to [Jesus] and begged him on his knees, "If you are willing, you can make me clean."
>
> Jesus was indignant. He reached out his hand and touched the man. "I am willing," he said. "Be clean!" Immediately the leprosy left him and he was cleansed.
>
> Jesus sent him away at once with a strong warning: "See that you don't tell this to anyone. But go, show yourself to the priest and offer the sacrifices that Moses commanded for your cleansing, as a testimony to them."

Imagine this story through the eyes of the leper.

Note your feelings at each point in the story.

Reflect on the importance of this having actually happened, first for the leper and second for you.

Reflect on times when God has clearly acted in your own life.

4. Think of the great and small acts of God recorded in the Bible. Focus on a few of them, and thank God for them.

5. Imagine Jesus sitting in a comfortable chair opposite you. Talk to him about your experience of God acting in your life. Tell him, too, about areas in which, despite praying, you don't see his action. Share your desires with him.

6. Conclude your time with this prayer:

> Go in peace to love and serve the Lord. In the name of Christ, Amen.

SUGGESTED ACTIVITIES

1. God's action in history is often shrouded in mystery. The major example of this in recent centuries is the Holocaust, in which some six million Jews and others were murdered in gas chambers. Where God

was in the midst of this evil is a great mystery. And yet some Christians found him amid that horror. Two examples are Corrie ten Boom and Etty Hillesum. Corrie survived; Etty did not. Read Corrie's *The Hiding Place* or watch the movie. Alternatively, read Etty's *An Interrupted Life*.[14]

2. Find a good timeline of the Bible and familiarize yourself with the main actors, events, and periods in the Bible's history.

---

14. Corrie ten Boom with Elizabeth Sherrill and John Sherrill, *The Hiding Place*, 35th anniversary edition (Grand Rapids: Chosen, 2006); Etty Hillesum, *An Interrupted Life*, trans. Arno Pomerans (New York: Pantheon, 1983).

7

KERYGMA

Eugene Peterson's translation of the Bible is titled *The Message*. This is an insightful title because the message of the Bible is what we are really after when we listen to it. Imagine you receive a letter from your boyfriend or girlfriend who is traveling for a year in Europe. It arrives months after they sent it and for some reason traveled halfway round the world before reaching you. There are many things you could do with it. You could, for example, use the various postal marks to reconstruct the journey it has been on. You could analyze the paper it is written on, try to work out if the style is the one you are familiar with, try to determine if it was all written at once, and so on. All of this could be interesting, but of course what you would surely do is to read it—again and again—to see what your boyfriend or girlfriend has to say to you through the letter. We might say that the goal of your reading is the message of the letter.

It is the same with the Bible. As noted earlier, in some churches the common practice after the Bible is read is for the reader to say, "This is the Word of the Lord," and for the congregation to respond, "Thanks be to God." I like this practice because it reminds us that the Bible is a message from God to us and that our goal in reading and studying the Bible must be to listen for and to that message.

I also like Peterson's title because it reminds us that the Bible ultimately speaks with one voice: *The Message*. As discussed in previous chapters, the primary author of the Bible is God, and God speaks with one true voice.

This is what we mean when we refer to the Bible as infallible. It is fully trustworthy as God's Word.

However, it is critical to note that this does not detract in any way from the thoroughly human nature of the Bible. It is written by many different human authors. This is why, when we speak of the inspiration of the Bible as God's Word written, we speak of its organic inspiration. The Bible was neither dropped from heaven nor dictated by God. God supervised the Bible's writing over hundreds of years in ancient cultures—through his sojourn with Old Testament Israel and climaxing in the Christ event—so that it is truly human but also truly God's Word.

The Threefold Cord

We have seen the importance of attending to three aspects of the Bible in particular: the literary, the historical, and the kerygmatic. Indeed, in the previous chapter we saw how the literary and the historical are so deeply intertwined in Exodus 19–24 that in order to grasp the one we have to take account of the other. The same is true of the message—or what I prefer to call the kerygmatic dimension of the Bible. *Kērygma* is the Greek word for "message," and the message is above all what we are after when we read the Bible.

The Bible is a religious book in that its primary concern is to tell us about God, the world, and ourselves. Thus, we will misunderstand it if we treat it as primarily a history book or a literary book. As we have seen, part of what it does is tell us about events that took place, and in this sense it is indeed historical. The way in which it does this is through literary texts, so the Bible is indeed literature. But both its historical and literary dimensions are in the service of its kerygma; they are subordinate to it. When it comes to the threefold cord, the kerygmatic is the dominant strand. As we saw with Exodus 19–24, to access the kerygma we have to work through the literary and the historical but always with a view to the text's message. Because the Bible is a religious book, its texts are intentionally shaped in this way.

Reading for the Message

The World Opened Up in Front of the Text

When interpreting the Bible, there are few more important matters to be clear on than why we are reading. As the saying goes, if you aim for nothing, you are bound to hit it. What exactly should we aim for in our work on the Bible? Obviously, we want to read for its message, but this is complex and nuanced. The message of the Bible is not like a text message! The Bible is made up of sixty-six books, a variety of genres, two Testaments, and so on. We do well to think through carefully just what is involved in reading for the message. We will use two approaches to answer this question.

First, we will use the approach of the French philosopher Paul Ricoeur (1913–2005). Ricoeur makes three helpful distinctions:

- The world of/in the text
- The world behind the text
- The world opened up in front of the text

It is worth observing how Ricoeur uses the metaphor of a "world" to explain what happens when we read a text. The world of/in the text is very much what we have called the literary nature of the text. It includes things like the main characters, the plot, the different acts, and scenes or episodes. The world behind the text is what we have called the historical aspect. It is that to which the text refers. Where Ricoeur is very helpful and insightful is in his emphasis on the world in front of the text, which is a sophisticated way of referring to what we call the message.

Ricoeur argues that when readers engage with a text, a world opens up in front of the text, which the reader is invited to indwell. This is extremely helpful when it comes to the books of the Bible. Think, for example, of our discussion of Luke's Gospel in chapter 5. Luke refers to actual events, and the book is a carefully crafted literary whole. In other words, there is a complex shape to the surface of the text. As the reader engages with Luke, paying close attention to its literary shape, a world is opened up in which events among the first-century Judean Jews are shown to have universal implications. The reader, as Ricoeur puts it, is invited to indwell that world, and such indwelling is potentially transformative.

Ricoeur's approach is helpful in many ways. It reminds us that even if we have worked hard on the historicity of the text (the world behind the text) and on the literary shape of the text (the world of the text), we have by no means completed the interpretive task. Analysis of these worlds must be in the service of the world opened up in front of the text. Second, Ricoeur's approach reminds us that the message of the Bible and its individual books cannot be reduced to propositions. Certainly there will be truths embedded in the world opened up in front of the text, which we can extract and analyze, but if we focus on propositions alone, we will, as Kevin Vanhoozer puts it, catch only half the fish,[1] if we are lucky. Literary texts require the full engagement of the imagination as well as the cognition or mind, and we will have to think and imagine ourselves in the position of someone like Theophilus as he read Luke in order to indwell the world opened up. Third, once we recognize that the Bible is not just another literary text but the living Word of God, then the transformative potential is wonderfully enhanced. With Luke, for example, we are called to attend to the text so that more and more the world is opened up in front of it, and to indwell it, and to allow it to do its transformative work on us. Fourth, we need to remember that we have to attend ultimately not just to the world opened up by individual biblical texts but to the world opened up by the entire Bible. Using Ricoeur's language, we might say that the worlds opened up by the individual books interact with one another—the word for this is *intertextuality*—to open up for us a world in front of the Bible as a whole.[2]

The Rhetorical Trajectory of the Text

Our second way to get at what it means to read for the message is reading for the rhetorical trajectory of the text. By *rhetorical* here we mean the communicative trajectory of the text. Rhetoric, which has a long history, studies the ways in which a text communicates and persuades. With some biblical texts this is obvious. Take the letters in the New Testament, for example. They are letters to first-century congregations, and we need to read them to hear what Paul or John or Peter or the author of Hebrews was saying to their recipients. The communicative trajectory is out in the open. However, when it comes to historical narrative, we too easily miss the rhetorical trajectory. Let me provide several examples.

1 and 2 Kings

First and Second Kings tell the story of the monarchy in Israel. The history is complex, and we might think, as some commentaries do, that once

---

1. Kevin J. Vanhoozer, *The Drama of Doctrine: A Canonical Linguistic Approach to Christian Theology* (Philadelphia: Westminster John Knox, 2005), 288.
2. See chap. 2 in this respect.

we have tackled this history we have done our work. An effect of historical criticism has been to challenge the story told by such books again and again. As a result, understandably, many evangelicals have seen their main task as defending the historicity of such books. Well and good; this is important work, but it does not complete the interpretive task.

The key to moving to the rhetorical trajectory with historical narrative is to realize that, even when we are not sure exactly when a book was written or precisely for whom, the one thing we can be sure about is that such books were *not* written for the people referred to in the book.[3] For example, 1 and 2 Kings were written for Israelites who lived after the events and people they refer to—that is, they were written for a people either in exile or/and back in the land but without a king. In my opinion, the interpretive key to 1 and 2 Kings is 2 Kings 17, which explains in detail why the Northern Kingdom went into exile. Second Kings 17:19 also says the Southern Kingdom was guilty of the same sins as the Northern Kingdom. This can be diagrammatically represented as follows:

FIGURE 7.1

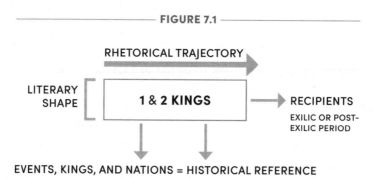

Thus, if we want to get at the rhetorical trajectory of 1 and 2 Kings, we have to imagine ourselves in exile or in the postexilic period and ask what these books would say to us in "our" depleted situation without a king. Among other things, they tell us why there is no longer a king and why God sent first the Northern Kingdom and then the Southern Kingdom into exile, thereby showing readers the importance of obeying God today lest they incur his wrath in their situation. As dreadful as exile was, 1 and 2 Kings

---

3. This is not to deny that sometimes/often we can infer the message to the people involved in the story told. We will see this, e.g., with Jeremiah's letter to the exiles discussed in chap. 12.

also make unequivocally clear that it was God who sent the Israelites into exile and not the gods of Assyria and Babylon. God is neither a national nor a territorial God but the one who rules over all nations, and this means that there is hope for the future.

Jonah

A second example is the prophetic narrative of Jonah, already discussed above. As a narrative, Jonah is unique in the Book of the Twelve, the Minor Prophets. For two reasons it took me years to learn how to listen to Jonah. In my early seminary training, study of Jonah was dominated by the question, Is it historical or not? For many this was and is a litmus test of evangelical orthodoxy, and thus our studies were consumed with this question. We will not try to solve that issue here, other than to note from chapter 6 that the key is the intention of the author and whether or not he intended the book to be historical. For our purposes, it is important to remember that solving this issue one way or another contributes little to our listening to the message of Jonah.

The second obstacle to my listening to Jonah was that it was common to leap straight to the New Testament where Jesus uses Jonah as a type of himself and then to argue that Jonah is about Jesus. Again, the relationship between Jonah and Jesus is an important issue, but clearly the book of Jonah meant something to its hearers centuries before Jesus came on the scene. If we are to access its message, then it is vital that we ask how its original hearers would have heard the message. The rhetorical trajectory again becomes the key as set out below.

———————————— FIGURE 7.2 ————————————

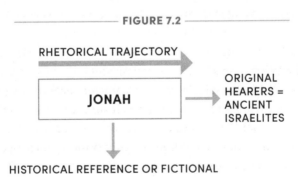

We do not know when or by whom Jonah was written. Nevertheless, it is when we imagine ourselves as a group of Israelites listening to this story that it really comes alive. Jonah is a gripping narrative and carefully crafted literature. It is through close attention to its poetics that we arrive at the kerygma, the world opened up in front of the text—or the rhetorical trajectory.

The opening words—"The word of the LORD came to"—would immediately have identified Jonah as a prophet. Jonah son of Amittai is known in the Old Testament from 2 Kings 14:25 as a prophet who brought good news to a bad northern king—Jeroboam II—about his restoring the boundaries of Israel. Whether Jonah is historical narrative or fiction, we should certainly imagine Jonah as the Jonah of 2 Kings 14:25. Doubtless his prophecy was well received in royal circles. Now God's word comes to him again, but nothing could prepare Jonah—or the audience—for the shocking commission he receives: Go to Nineveh. Nineveh was the capital of Assyria, a great enemy of Israel and the nation that took the Northern Kingdom into exile. You can imagine the Israelite audience of the book of Jonah sitting on the edge of their seats—after picking themselves up from the floor!—to see what Jonah will do.

The Hebrew has a play on words that does not come out in the NIV. God commands Jonah to "arise," . . . and Jonah "arose." Is he going to rise to the challenge? On the contrary. He arises . . . to flee to Tarshish in Spain, diametrically away from Nineveh and hopefully far from God's presence. Listening to Jonah as though among a group of Israelites is wonderfully illuminating. Jonah cannot escape from YHWH's presence; YHWH pursues him. Jonah's disobedience brings God's wrath on innocent sailors, who behave more like true Israelites than the prophet Jonah. God works to bring Jonah to Nineveh, and remarkably the Ninevites repent. God relents of his judgment on them, making Jonah very angry. God provides a bush to shade Jonah from the heat, and when it withers, Jonah requests to die.

In one sense Jonah is a bad, incomplete story. It ends with a poignant question: "But the LORD said, 'You have been concerned about this plant, though you did not tend it or make it grow. It sprang up overnight and died overnight. And should I not have concern for the great city of Nineveh, in which there are more than a hundred and twenty thousand people who cannot tell their right hand from their left—and also many animals?'" (4:10–11).

The story is left incomplete; we are never told how Jonah responds to the question. This confirms what we have been sensing as the story is told: it's not finally about Jonah but about us. Listening as Israelites, we—like

Jonah—bear the word of God. Are we willing to be compassionate to our enemies like God, or do we remain angry like Jonah? Here we see how the historical and the literary dimensions of the text serve its kerygma.

Listened to like this, the kerygma of Jonah is exceptionally powerful. Its rhetorical trajectory lands in our midst like a bomb, as we realize that the story is about us. It is we who are called to become like God. We are made in his image (Gen. 1:26–28), but we need to become what we are by creation.

Genesis 1–2

A third example is that of Genesis 1–2. As with Jonah, it took me years after seminary before I felt I could preach this great and foundational text. Why? Once again my seminary work on this text was consumed with historical and scientific questions. We focused on questions like, Are the days twenty-four-hour days or not? Does Genesis 1–2 teach creationism? How do science and evolution relate to these opening chapters of the Bible? In other words, we prioritized our own modern questions in reading these chapters rather than first exploring their rhetorical trajectory for their original hearers. The scientific questions are important, but Darwin propounded his theory of evolution in the nineteenth century, so there is no way the early hearers of Genesis 1 and 2 would have had such questions in mind.

We do not know when or by whom Genesis 1–2 was written. It is carefully crafted literature, perhaps by an author steeped in the wisdom tradition,[4] and would have been written sometime during the history of Israel. Of course, no human was present during creation, so one thing we can rule out is that Genesis 1–2 contains eyewitness testimony to what God actually did! Creation is *sui generis*; it is unlike any other event since it is what makes events in our world possible. Genesis 1 and 2 bear witness to creation, and what an extraordinarily rich and powerful witness it is. Once again, how do we listen to these chapters so that we can hear their powerful testimony?

As with 1–2 Kings and Jonah, the rhetorical trajectory is the key. We have to imagine ourselves back in the minds and lives of the Israelites and ask how they would have heard these creation narratives. Our questions tend to be scientific; theirs were not. However, they did have their own questions. The ancient Near East was thoroughly polytheistic, full of

4. Henri Blocher, *In the Beginning: The Opening Chapters of Genesis*, trans. David G. Preston (Downers Grove, IL: InterVarsity, 1984), 34.

gods and full of different creation stories. You simply could not have lived in Egypt or in Canaan without being aware of such stories, and naturally you would wonder how YHWH relates to such stories. From archaeological discoveries we now know a great deal about the creation stories of the nations surrounding Israel, and it is particularly when read against their background that Genesis 1 and 2 speak most powerfully.

First, Genesis 1 only knows of one God, "Elohim," and everything that comes into existence does so through his work and at his command. This may strike us as so obvious as to be insignificant, but such monotheism (one God) was virtually unheard of in the ancient Near East and would have spoken powerfully among cultures with hundreds of gods. The name for God in Genesis 1:1–2:3 is "Elohim," which is plural in form. However the verbs accompanying it are singular, so there is no suggestion here of multiple gods. The plural is probably a plural of majesty, appropriately evoking God as the majestic Creator King. He is royalty par excellence. Genesis 2:4–3:24 uses an unusual name for God: "YHWH Elohim" ("LORD God"). YHWH is the name of God particularly associated with the exodus and the events at Sinai (see Exod. 3 and 6). The unusual and deliberate juxtaposition of YHWH and Elohim reminds Israelite readers that the God who rescued them from slavery and brought them to himself at Sinai is the Creator God. As YHWH says in Exodus 19:5, the whole earth belongs to him!

In the ancient Near East the gods were part of the world. Not so Elohim. He is apart from the world—his transcendence—and he speaks the entire creation into existence. Remember that "heaven and earth" in 1:1 refers to the whole of the creation by referring to its two extremities (a merism). It is Genesis's way of saying what John says in John 1:3: "Through him all things were made; without him nothing was made that has been made."

Once we attend to Genesis 1 and 2 in terms of its rhetorical trajectory for the Israelites, a colossal view of God emerges, something that we easily miss when we approach these texts first with our modern questions. And this Creator God is none other than the God who has brought us to himself. So great is God that we might think he utterly transcends the creation, but this is not the case. He takes great interest in forming the creation from its formless state into its differentiated shape. In Genesis 1:26–28 we read about humans being created in God's image, and in Genesis 2:4–25 the focus narrows to the home of the first couple in that great park of Eden. We see in this chapter how God is deeply and immanently involved in and with his creation.

If a colossal view of God emerges from Genesis 1–2, likewise a fascinating view of what it means to be human comes to the fore. In Egypt the pharaoh was thought to be a god and in the image of the gods. Here in Genesis 1:26–28, the image is democratized; every human bears the image of God and as such is called to royal service in his creation. Accompanying an extraordinary view of God, we find a creaturely and wonderfully dignified view of the human person—and not just of the Israelite but of all humans.

Israel's history was tumultuous, full of wars and rebellion. It is amazing that out of such a history a text like Genesis 1:1–2:3 should emerge with its insistence that all creation is good, indeed very good. Genesis delivers a wonderfully positive view of the world and every aspect of it: land, sea, sky, and the multitude of different creatures that fill these major spaces. Genesis affirms the goodness of creation even while demythologizing it. What I mean by that is this. For the nations of the ancient Near East, the world was filled with gods; the sun was commonly thought to be a god, as were certain animals, the moon, and the stars. Genesis will have none of this. For example, on the fourth day, God makes the greater light and the lesser light—that is, the sun and the moon. In Hebrew there are words for "sun" and "moon," but the author does not use them. Why? Most probably in order to remind the reader that they are God's creation and not gods.

Once we approach Genesis 1–2 in this way, we start to access its powerful message. It is material that can and must be preached. Here in Genesis are the building blocks of a Christian worldview, and such massive building blocks—far more impressive than the great pyramids of Egypt—need to be announced again and again to every new generation.

New Testament

As our fourth and final example, we will look at some New Testament books. We have already noted that the communicative trajectory of the New Testament letters is clear and easy to identify. One reason for this is that, unlike in the Gospels and other historical narrative, the readers are identified in the letters themselves. The result is that the communicative trajectory is on the surface. A challenge with letters, however, is that we are sometimes listening to only one side of the conversation and thus need to be aware that there are things we do not know. This is particularly true of 1 and 2 Corinthians, where Paul addresses the many problems in the church in Corinth, but we generally don't know the details of the problems.

The authors of the New Testament letters develop this genre to fit their purposes. This is particularly clear in Romans and Hebrews, where the letter form is massively expanded to allow for extensive and deep instruction about the gospel. The Gospels likewise are written so as to lend themselves to a wide audience. Nevertheless, in all cases a sense of the rhetorical trajectory remains helpful. The view that the Gospels were written for very particular communities has been widely criticized,[5] but as we saw with Luke, it can still be helpful to try indwelling the world they open up for us. One thing we know, as with 1 and 2 Kings, is that the Gospels were not written for the people referred to in them but for later Christians. Furthermore, Matthew was probably written for a predominantly Jewish audience, which accounts for his great stress on how Jesus fulfills the Old Testament and for his use of "kingdom of heaven" rather than the other Gospels' "kingdom of God," as discussed earlier. When it comes to the letters, it is important to listen to them as their early hearers would have heard them.

We've already discussed the importance of Romans and Hebrews among the New Testament letters, and they provide good examples here as well. Romans was written by Paul to prepare the way for his planned visit to the church in Rome. Hebrews was written to predominantly Jewish Christians who were tempted to lapse into the kind of Judaism from which they had been converted. In both letters the good news of Jesus is unpacked in great depth. The different ways in which this is done are noteworthy. It is the same good news of Jesus that is front and center, but whereas in Hebrews it is unpacked using images from the sacrificial system (cultus), in Romans legal metaphors dominate.

Romans and Hebrews do not contradict each other, but they are markedly different. What the differences show us is that the good news of Jesus is extraordinarily rich, and it can be expounded for different audiences in a variety of ways—one way for the Romans, another for the Hebrews.

Conclusion

In our approach to the Bible, we want to find ourselves saying with Samuel, "Speak, LORD, for your servant is listening" (1 Sam. 3:9), and with Mary, "I am the Lord's servant. May your word to me be fulfilled" (Luke 1:38). It is

5. See Richard Bauckham, ed., *The Gospels for All Christians: Rethinking the Gospel Audiences* (Grand Rapids: Eerdmans, 1998).

the work of the Spirit to open us to God through the Bible. However, such inspiration is by no means opposed to perspiration, and we need to do all we can to listen to the Bible in such a way that the accompanying work of the Spirit becomes most likely.

In this chapter and the previous two, we have considered the nature of the biblical text—its threefold cord of literary, historical, and kerygmatic dimensions. We simply must attend to them and their interrelationship if we want to do justice to the Bible. The historical thread is most pronounced in the historical narratives, though it is also present in different ways in books like the Old Testament Wisdom literature and the letters of the New Testament. The historical narratives do tell us about what happened, but they are also literature, and both the historical and literary threads in our cord are always in the service of the kerygma, the dominant thread in our threefold cord.

I have focused in this chapter on letting our hard work on the Bible culminate in the world opened up in front of the text—the rhetorical trajectory. The message is what we are after, and just as the Bible makes the historical and the literary subservient to the kerygma, so, too, we must ensure that our historical and literary analysis is always headed toward and in service of the text's message.

The perceptive reader will note that I have stressed that we do this by taking seriously how the Bible's early readers would have heard it in their particular contexts. This is what Brevard Childs means when he insists that we must attend to the discrete witness of the biblical books. But, of course, we are neither ancient Israelites nor members of the early church in Acts. The question thus arises, How do we listen to God's Word for us today? If we want to listen and respond like Samuel and Mary, then this is a critical question, and it is the one we turn to in the next chapter.

DISCUSSION QUESTIONS

1. What do we mean by *kerygma*?
2. Do you agree that *The Message* is a great title for Eugene Peterson's translation of the Bible? Why or why not?
3. What do we mean by the rhetorical trajectory of a book? How does it help us listen to books like 1 and 2 Kings and Hebrews?

4. Do you find Paul Ricoeur's notion of the world opened up in front of the text helpful? Explain.

5. Why is "just" attending to the historical and literary dimensions of Jonah inadequate?

6. How does this chapter help you to discern the purpose of all your hard work on the Bible?

FURTHER READING

Bartholomew, Craig G., and David J. H. Beldman, eds. *Hearing the Old Testament: Listening for God's Address*. Grand Rapids: Eerdmans, 2012. This book is unique in making the kerygma—listening for God's address—the focus of all the essays.

Green, Joel B., ed. *Hearing the New Testament: Strategies for Interpretation*. 2nd ed. Grand Rapids: Eerdmans, 2010. See especially chapters 1 and 13.

"Kerygma." In *The Baker Illustrated Bible Dictionary*, edited by Tremper Longman III, 1000. Grand Rapids: Baker Books, 2013.

DEVOTIONAL EXERCISE

1. Kerygma reminds us that God speaks. To hear him we need to listen. Set your concerns aside, and take five minutes to come to stillness before God, saying, "Speak, Lord, for your servant is listening."

2. Read the following passage carefully, several times.

Matthew 1:18–25

This is how the birth of Jesus the Messiah came about: His mother Mary was pledged to be married to Joseph, but before they came together, she was found to be pregnant through the Holy Spirit. Because Joseph her husband was faithful to the law, and yet did not want to expose her to public disgrace, he had in mind to divorce her quietly.

But after he had considered this, an angel of the Lord appeared to him in a dream and said, "Joseph son of David, do not be afraid to take Mary home as your wife, because what is conceived in her is from the Holy Spirit. She will give birth to a son, and you are to give him the name Jesus, because he will save his people from their sins."

All this took place to fulfill what the Lord had said through the prophet: "The virgin will conceive and give birth to a son, and they will call him Immanuel" (which means "God with us").

When Joseph woke up, he did what the angel of the Lord had commanded him and took Mary home as his wife. But he did not consummate their marriage until she gave birth to a son. And he gave him the name Jesus.

Put yourself in Joseph's shoes. How are you feeling at the news that Mary is pregnant?

What transforms his situation?

Why is it so important that Joseph listened to God?

Are there situations you are facing in which you need to listen to God?

3. Imagine Jesus sitting opposite you. Speak to him about your reactions to the story you have just read. Are you facing situations in which you need to hear God speaking? Tell Jesus about them.

4. If you are facing specific situations in which you need to hear God speak, make a note of them in a journal. Then, as you wait on God, when he responds, you can return to your journal and record his communication with you.

5. Give thanks that Joseph listened to God. Think back to situations where you have done the same, and rejoice.

6. Conclude your time with this prayer from Hebrews 13:20–21:

Now may the God of peace, who through the blood of the eternal covenant brought back from the dead our Lord Jesus, that great Shepherd of the sheep, equip you with everything good for doing his will, and may he work in us what is pleasing to him, through Jesus Christ, to whom be glory for ever and ever. Amen.

SUGGESTED ACTIVITIES

1. Gather together a group of your friends or classmates. Appoint a good speaker to read aloud the story of Jonah. As a group imagine that you are Old Testament Israelites whose great enemy is Assyria. After you have listened to the story, share your insights.

2. Although we don't do this often anymore, it can be a fun exercise: Handwrite a letter to a close friend or family member who lives some distance away. Choose the paper and envelope carefully, and see if the post office has an interesting stamp to use when you mail it. Ask the friend/family member to do the same to you.

   Enjoy the experience of waiting for their letter to arrive. When it does, savor it. Examine the envelope, paper, and stamps to see if they enhance the letter.

   As you reflect on this experience, ask yourself, Above all else why did I read the letter?

8

LISTENING TO AND PREACHING THE BIBLE TODAY

In his marvelous book *Under the Gaze of the Bible*, the French, Catholic philosopher Jean-Louis Chrétien begins with a chapter titled "Reading the Bible Today." He proposes that we let the Bible define for us the meaning of *today*, and in this respect he turns to Hebrews 3:7–11, which quotes Psalm 95:

> So, as the Holy Spirit says:
> "**Today**, if you hear his voice,
>   do not harden your hearts
> as you did in the rebellion,
>   during the time of testing in the wilderness,
> where your ancestors tested and tried me,
>   though for forty years they saw what I did.
> That is why I was angry with that generation;
>   I said, 'Their hearts are always going astray,
>   and they have not known my ways.'
> So I declared on oath in my anger,
>   'They shall never enter my rest.'" (emphasis added)

According to Chrétien, the "today" of Psalm 95 and Hebrews 3 becomes "our own today when we read [the Bible] in order to listen."[1] The today of

---

1. Jean-Louis Chrétien, *Under the Gaze of the Bible*, trans. John Marson Dunaway (New York: Fordham University Press, 2015), 2.

such an opportunity will not last forever. It is therefore urgent—as Psalm 95 makes clear—that we read the Bible to listen. Chrétien notes that Augustine compared the Bible to personal letters sent to us, and he writes, "When I read the Bible in this way and receive it as a missive in which my name is traced with the sympathetic ink of grace, the today of my living attention enters the temporal dimension of which this writing itself speaks, that is, the sacred story."[2]

I love Chrétien's evocative style. Let me explain how I understand him. In philosophical hermeneutics[3] many of the big issues of life are explored—issues like history, time, language, and how humans understand. These are complex issues, but it is important to realize that the Bible already provides us with a framework for understanding them. It is not a theoretical, philosophical framework—I would call it pretheoretical or a worldview—but it is a framework, nevertheless. For the Bible, time and thus history are part of God's good creation, and there is a telos to history, when Christ will return and the kingdom of God will finally and fully come. Both Jews and Christians look for God's kingdom to come in history. A crucial difference is that Christians believe the kingdom of God has already come in Christ but is still to be fully consummated.[4] Our "today" is thus the time between the coming of the kingdom and its final consummation. This, as we saw in chapter 2, is act 5 of the great drama of Scripture, the era of mission.

Thus, as we think of listening to the Bible, the Bible itself already goes a long way toward defining our "today." As we saw in chapter 2, although we do not live in acts 3, 4, or 6 of the great drama, we are called to use all the insights we can from all the acts of the Bible in order to hear and obey God today.

The Concrete Reality of God's Word

As is typical of the prophetic books, Amos begins by telling us about the precise time when the prophet was prophesying: "The words of Amos, one

2. Chrétien, *Under the Gaze of the Bible*, 2–3.
3. See "The Role of Hermeneutics" in chap. 1 above.
4. See the excellent work by E. Earle Ellis, "The New Testament's Use of the Old Testament," in *Biblical Hermeneutics: A Comprehensive Introduction to Interpreting Scripture*, ed. B. Corley, Steve W. Lemke, and Grant I. Lovejoy, 2nd ed. (Nashville: Broadman & Holman, 2002), 72–89, esp. 83.

of the shepherds of Tekoa—the vision he saw concerning Israel two years before the earthquake, when Uzziah was king of Judah and Jeroboam son of Jehoash was king of Israel" (1:1).

This verse tells us important information about Amos. The word for "shepherd" probably means more of a landowner and businessman than what we typically think of as a shepherd. Tekoa was in the Southern Kingdom of Judah, whereas Amos prophesied to the Northern Kingdom, Israel.[5] We know that Amos lived and prophesied during act 3 of the great drama of Scripture—when God chooses Israel—but this verse enables us to be far more specific. Amos ministered after Israel had broken up into a southern kingdom—Judah—and a northern kingdom—Israel. When he prophesied, Uzziah was king of the Southern Kingdom (790–740 BC) and Jeroboam II was king over the north (786–746 BC). The reference to "the earthquake" locates Amos's ministry even more precisely, and certainly it would have meant something significant to the hearers of this book.

What do we learn from this? Many things, but what is significant for our purposes is that God's Word always comes to his people in their specific context. It comes to them in their particular "today." As Martin Buber notes, "Every prophet speaks in the actuality of a definite situation. The situation, however, serves the prophet not only as a starting point, but he throws the word of God into this actuality according to His injunctions, and only if we try ourselves to delve into this actuality, can we grasp the concrete reality of the word."[6] God's Word comes into the concrete reality of the lives of his people, into their immediate context. This means that when it comes to the Bible, as Buber notes, to hear it we have to delve into the concrete realities in which God originally spoke his Word. This is why in the previous chapter we stressed the importance of taking seriously the discrete witness of the biblical texts, asking how the original hearers would have heard the message.

However, when we listen to the Bible, our goal is to hear what God is saying to us today. Thus, a crucial part of interpreting the Bible is making the connection between the discrete witness of the biblical texts and their message for today.

---

5. See Craig G. Bartholomew and Heath A. Thomas, *The Minor Prophets: A Theological Introduction* (Downers Grove, IL: IVP Academic, 2023).

6. Martin Buber, *The Prophetic Faith* (New York: Harper & Row, 1949), 96.

Our Concrete Reality

As noted above, we already know a great deal about our own context. We are in act 5 of the great drama of Scripture. We are not part of the theocratic nation of Israel, which was in a covenant with God as a nation. We are part of the church, the people of God scattered among the nations in this age of mission. In this respect we share a great deal with the churches we read about in the New Testament; we live in the same act as they did.

Yet our concrete situations are very different from those of the early Christians. Let me provide a few examples. We read the Bible in a printed book or online, perhaps on our smart phones. The early church adopted the codex, so written copies of the Gospels and other parts of the Bible were more readily available than we might think. Nevertheless, we live on the other side of the printing revolution and in a technological revolution—both of which were, of course, completely unknown to the early church. Most early Christians would have listened to Scripture read in a group, while we tend to read it from one of many translations available either in print or online.

In the West and many other parts of the world, we live in democracies, a form of government unknown to the early church. The authority of Caesar was absolute in the Roman Empire, so the early Christians would be unfamiliar with political freedoms we take for granted. Of course, if you live in Russia or North Korea, you may experience authoritarian situations much closer to that of the early church. Our capitalist economies function very differently from the economies of the Roman Empire, as does the way we work—normally in offices that are separate from our homes, although the pandemic has affected that. In the West we generally have separate church buildings where we meet for worship, a phenomenon unknown in the early church. For the most part, we go to schools for our education. Even home schooling is "school," in the sense that a curriculum covering all the basics is required. In the first century, by comparison, most education took place in the home. And so we could continue. The main point is clear: our concrete reality is often very different from that of the early church.

When Mike Goheen and I wrote *Living at the Crossroads: An Introduction to Christian Worldview*,[7] I vividly recall writing parts of the final sec-

---

7. Michael W. Goheen and Craig G. Bartholomew, *Living at the Crossroads: An Introduction to Christian Worldview* (Grand Rapids: Baker Academic, 2008).

tion, which contains vignettes about how a Christian worldview relates to contemporary subjects. I was struck repeatedly with the importance of knowing the history of a subject or an area of life if we are to relate the Bible and a biblical worldview to them. Knowing, for example, how politics has developed over the centuries is invaluable in working out how the Bible might relate to politics today. Likewise with the family. I have on my shelves a large book on the history of domesticity and how family life has changed and evolved over the centuries. Such awareness provides critical perspective on how we practice domesticity today and goes a long way toward helping us apply nuanced insights about family life from the Bible.

Another way to get at the difference between the early church and us is to attend to the problems Paul and the other apostles address in their letters. Take Galatians 1:11–2:21, for example. Clearly the apostleship of Paul had become a problem in Galatia; hence Paul's long discussion of his apostleship and defense of his authority. In most of our churches, Paul's authority is not a problem. We accept that his letters are a vital part of Holy Scripture. How then do we listen to such a passage today?

The church in Corinth had many problems, such as lawsuits among fellow believers (1 Cor. 6:1–11), whether or not to eat food offered to idols (1 Cor. 8), the use of head coverings by women (1 Cor. 11:1–16), and whether or not the dead rise (1 Cor. 15:12). Our churches may struggle with some of these problems, in which case the text may speak directly to them. We saw this, for example, with the resurrection in chapter 6 above. However, it is unlikely that we struggle with issues such as food offered to idols, although some cultures today do struggle with such issues. How, though, do we listen to passages that address problems we do not have today?

Such differences are not necessarily bad; often they are very good. Cultures—the way in which we organize our societies—develop, and part of what Christian scholars do is to assess the merits and negative aspects of such cultural development. It is, for example, a great thing that the Bible is so readily available in so many different languages today. And who among us would prefer to live in an authoritarian country rather than a democracy?

However, what these differences mean is that there is work to be done to move from the discrete witness of the Bible to what God is saying to us today.

The Clarity of Scripture

Before we attend to the move from the discrete witness of the Bible to hearing it today, we should note that the move is immediate for much of Scripture. Indeed, the doctrine of the clarity of Scripture, as discussed earlier in this book, says that much of the Bible is clear and not hard to understand or relate to our lives today. You do not, for example, need to engage in sophisticated hermeneutics to understand that the great story of the Bible climaxes in Jesus, rather than in any current political leader. This is right on the surface of the Bible; it couldn't be clearer. The same is true of many ethical issues. Most of the Ten Commandments relate immediately to our lives today. No sophistication is required to know that murder is wrong, nor do we have to struggle to understand that God does not approve of adultery. Likewise, false testimony in a legal context is almost always wrong.

However, "clarity" is a metaphor, and when it is brought together with "Scripture," it sparks the insight that much in the Bible is clear, but *also that much remains unclear*. This is, after all, why churches have pastors and teachers. In each generation their role is to devote themselves to the Word and prayer and to keep pulling back the curtain of Scripture, so that more and more of the Bible becomes clear to us today.

Consider some of the laws in the Pentateuch, for example. It is very clear in the Pentateuch that God instructs his people how to live, but some of the details are far from clear to us. Exodus 23:19 is an extreme example: "Do not cook a young goat in its mother's milk." Even taking the context into account, it is hard to know precisely what this law is about. The instruction is clear, but the motivation is not. To begin to make sense of such a law, we have to refer to the discrete witness of Exodus and ask what this might have meant to the Israelites. Obviously, it is part of Israel's many dietary laws. Background knowledge of the cultures around Israel may also help. But even so sophisticated a Jewish commentator as Nahum Sarna says of this verse that it "largely remains an enigma."[8]

It is particularly important when we read parts of the Bible that are unclear or take place in acts other than our own that we first ask, What did this passage mean to its original hearers? before we ask, What does this passage mean to us today? The previous chapter has several examples of just how

8. Nahum Sarna, *Exodus*, JPS Torah Commentary (Jerusalem: Jewish Publication Society, 1991), 147.

illuminating this can be. For example, our questions about science and origins in relation to Genesis 1–2 are important, but we skew and obfuscate the witness of these chapters if we don't first ask how the Israelites would have heard them and, only then, what they say to us today.

Double Listening

The great John Stott coined the term *double listening*. By this he meant that if we are to listen to the Bible, we need to have one ear in the Bible and one ear in our contemporary culture(s). One of the most penetrating insights of modern hermeneutics is that readers of the Bible in the twenty-first century are as much embedded in history as are the biblical authors and texts. Thus, we listen out of our particular contexts, as a man or a woman, as a Welshman or an American, as a person of color or white, as highly educated or not, as part of a particular church with its own traditions, and so on. Just as we need to understand the story of the Bible, so we need to be intimately acquainted with the stories of our cultures, with the worldviews that surround us. Only in this way will we be strongly positioned to listen to what God is saying to us today, so that the Word can penetrate as deeply into our concrete reality as it did with the prophets and apostles. We have seen, for example, how Paul addresses the problems the Corinthian Christians were struggling with. Their problems may not be ours, but we have our own problems, and the better we understand them, the better we can see how the Bible addresses them.

If this is true at a personal and church level, it is also true at a cultural level. The Bible addresses all of life, but in order to hear its full acoustics, we need to know the challenges of our day. What, we might ask, are the biggest challenges facing Western culture? What are the biggest challenges of our churches? What are our biggest personal challenges? We need to think hard about such issues and read widely. John Stott, for example, made it a practice to go with friends to see the latest films and discuss them afterward in order to be as in touch as possible with contemporary culture.

Two Trajectories and the Bible's Message

The Word arrives powerfully in our concrete realities at the intersection of two trajectories. The first is the rhetorical trajectory of the book or passage we are reading. The second is the trajectory emerging from our own lives, churches, cultures, and contexts. It is when these intersect that the explosion of the good news of the Bible takes place.

This is true individually as well as for preaching.[9] Evangelicals are well known for launching their sermons from the Bible. Alas, far too often they are aimed nowhere in particular. Liberals, by comparison, shoot their sermons right into the contemporary world. Alas, far too often we are not sure where the sermon has come from! If, as John Stott argued, what we want in our pulpits is truth on fire, then we need sermons that come right out of the Bible and explode in our particular, concrete realities.

Or think of the sermon as a plane carrying the precious cargo of the Word. Sometimes a sermon endlessly circles above but never actually lands in a particular congregation. What we need are sermons that, Sunday after Sunday, land the life-giving cargo of the Word right in the middle of the congregation. This is why churches appoint pastors, who, as Eugene Peterson so eloquently points out, have the awesome responsibility of keeping God's people attentive to God.[10] But a pastor is not called to serve just any of God's people, but a very particular flock. If pastors are doing their work well and immersing themselves in the daily lives of their flocks, they will discover the particular challenges of their people. And it is to those people that they are called to preach the Word. It is particular congregations with particular strengths and weaknesses that pastors are to keep attentive to God.

The sermon should take shape at the intersection of these two trajectories. Sometimes homileticians say that you must discern the telos or trajectory of the text, and that is what you must preach. In my view this is only half of the picture and easily prevents the sermon from penetrating the concrete, daily realities of the congregation. Let me provide some examples.

We saw how in Galatians 1:11–2:21 Paul defends his apostolic authority. How do you preach such a text in a church where no one doubts his apostolic authority? You could just preach the telos of the text, and doubtless this would serve as a healthy reminder to your congregation of Paul's apostleship and authority. However it would have nothing like its impact

9. Here I am adapting ideas from John Stott, *I Believe in Preaching*, rev. ed. (London: Hodder & Stoughton, 2014). See also Craig G. Bartholomew, *Excellent Preaching: Proclaiming the Gospel in Its Context and Ours* (Bellingham, WA: Lexham, 2015), for a far more detailed explanation of this approach.

10. Eugene Peterson, *Working the Angles: The Shape of Pastoral Integrity* (Grand Rapids: Eerdmans, 1987), 2.

in Galatia among Christians who really did doubt Paul's authority and were going astray as a result.

The trajectory of the text needs to be brought into conversation with the trajectory of your congregation. The following sort of questions need to be asked:

- What is apostolic authority, and why does it matter?
- What effect did questioning Paul's authority have on the church in Galatia?
- Are there analogous ways in which our cultures struggle with authority?
- Are there particular ways in which our congregation struggles with authority and specifically with the authority of the Bible?
- How do our churches and my congregation in particular go astray when biblical authority is subverted?

According to Ephesians 2:20, the church is built on the foundation of the apostles and the prophets with Christ as the cornerstone. Apostolic authority is all about authoritative testimony to the Christ event, and if this is lost, then the very foundations of the church begin to crumble. But churches lose this foundation in very different ways—the Galatians in one way, our twenty-first-century churches in others. We need to hear the message of Paul's apostleship in relation to the issues with which our culture and our churches struggle. It is this that needs to be proclaimed in the sermon, and thus the shape of the sermon will of necessity vary from congregation to congregation, and even within congregations over time. In my experience as a preacher, when these two trajectories are taken seriously, it is at their intersection that the shape of the sermon emerges.

When I was first ordained as an Anglican minister, I worked on the staff of a large evangelical church in South Africa. This was the time of apartheid South Africa, in which a vicious racism was legislated and practiced across the country in every area of life. The Nationalist government claimed to be Christian, and apartheid profoundly affected the lives of churches, which tended to be populated along racial lines. In my predominantly white church, you could be sure that racism existed not far below the respectable surface.

I preached a series through Ephesians, one of my favorite books. Ephesians may well have been written as a letter intended for circulation, and it certainly lacks the strong and specific rhetorical trajectory of Galatians.

I got to Ephesians 2:11–22, a text that is all about the unity of the church, how Jewish and gentile Christians are one in Christ. In Christ the wall of partition has been irrevocably shattered. We are so familiar with this idea that we often fail to realize how radical this message would have been in the early church. We know from Acts and Galatians that many early Jewish Christians struggled with this issue, doubtless often leaving gentile Christians feeling like second-class citizens. In its first-century context, Ephesians 2 would have spoken with exceptional power and clarity.

But how was I to preach it in my predominantly white evangelical church in South Africa? The issue of the relationship between Jewish and gentile Christians was simply not on our agenda. Thus, simply to preach the telos of the text would have been informative and interesting, but it would have had none of the penetration into our congregation's concrete reality that it would have had when it was read to the early Christians in Ephesus and other places. To preach this text with relevance and power, I needed to bring it into conversation with the trajectory of my congregation. Were there ways in which we struggled with the unity of the church? Were there ways in which we had erected barriers among the people of God in our locality and in South Africa as a whole?

As soon as I asked such questions, the answers were obvious. Apartheid divided not only the country but also the churches. And apart from what was going on in the country, congregations like mine needed to find ways to give expression to the unity of the church. It was at the intersection of the trajectories that my sermon took shape. Needless to say, many found the sermon disturbing, some labeled me a political preacher, and so on. One of the hardest things about being a pastor is that you are not called to give the sheep what they want, but what they need. And what they need is the Word contextualized in their concrete realities. It would have been a dreadful betrayal of my calling to preach this text and not land it amid the realities of apartheid South Africa.

In relation to this series on Ephesians, let me also mention how—in my youthful enthusiasm—I allowed a lack of awareness of my context to cause me to misread Ephesians 6 and thus serve my flock not nearly as well as I might have. Ephesians 6:10–17 is the famous passage on putting on the armor of God. I preached through this slowly, determined to have everyone in my flock decked out in the armor of God ready to go battle the forces of evil . . . alone! Reading the text through the eyes of Western individualism,

I failed to notice that the exhortations to put on the armor of God are all in the second-person plural! According to Paul, it is the congregation as a whole that is to put on the armor of God. No self-respecting soldier of the day would have dreamed of putting his armor on and then going out to face the enemy alone. The only hope of success was fighting together. As you will realize from my example above of Ephesians 2, the challenges to Christians in apartheid South Africa were considerable, far too great for the individual Christian to take on. Through inadvertently reading Ephesians 6 through an individualist lens, I failed my sheep.

Some readers may find this approach of two trajectories insightful but wonder if it is biblical. Is there any evidence, for example, that in the New Testament the Old Testament is read this way? This is a massive topic but an important one. I think the answer is yes; let me provide one example that is illuminating in all sorts of ways.

Imagine you are preaching through or reading Deuteronomy and you come across this text in Deuteronomy 25:4: "Do not muzzle an ox while it is treading out the grain." As a good Bible reader you might recall that Paul quotes this verse in 1 Corinthians 9:8–12:

Do I say this merely on human authority? Doesn't the Law say the same thing? For it is written in the Law of Moses: "Do not muzzle an ox while it is treading out the grain." Is it about oxen that God is concerned? Surely he says this for us, doesn't he? Yes, this was written for us, because whoever plows and threshes should be able to do so in the hope of sharing in the harvest. If we have sown spiritual seed among you, is it too much if we reap a material harvest from you? If others have this right of support from you, shouldn't we have it all the more?

If you neglect the discrete witness of the Old Testament, then you will simply read Deuteronomy 25:4 as about the worker being worthy of his hire. Apply it to ministers, and—with tongue in cheek—ask for a raise!

What does Deuteronomy 25:4 say in its Old Testament context? Craigie says that "it does not appear to have any particular relationship to its context."[11] On the surface this appears to be correct. The surrounding laws in Deuteronomy 24 and 25 all have to do with justice in human relationships.

11. Peter C. Craigie, *The Book of Deuteronomy*, New International Commentary on the Old Testament (Grand Rapids: Eerdmans, 1976), 313.

However, Thiselton says, "The unexpected insertion of one verse about threshing coheres most closely with the encouragement of human sensitivity and humane compassion toward the suffering or defenseless (e.g., the immediately preceding context concerns the plight of widows, orphans, and victims of punishment)."[12] If this is correct, then this verse is already being used in Deuteronomy in a way similar to that of 1 Corinthians—namely, relating the treatment of the ox to human relationships.

In his exegesis of this section in 1 Corinthians, Thistleton notes,

> Paul's question, then, **Is it perhaps about oxen that God is concerned?** (i.e., oxen *as such*) genuinely conveys the thrust of the context that constrains the force and direction of 25:4, although in this case it is more likely that μὴ . . . θεῷ is the μή used to express a *hesitant* question (**is it perhaps . . . ?**) rather than the question which invites an emphatically negative answer: *Surely God is not concerned for oxen, is he? Of course not!* . . . We may return to the excellent analysis by Hays, which receives some support from Straub, Fee, and others. Deut 25:4 "functions as an elegant metaphor for just the point that Paul wants to make: the ox being driven around and around on the threshing floor should not be cruelly restrained from eating the food that his own labor is making available . . . so, too, with apostles."[13]

Thus, even if in Deuteronomy 25:4 the injunction not to muzzle the ox is already being applied to human relationships, this does not for a moment detract from its application to how we treat our working animals. Indeed, if we attend to the discrete witness of this text, then it brings us onto the terrain of animal rights, a vital point that we easily ignore if we read Deuteronomy 25:4 through the lens of 1 Corinthians 9. We know from texts like Jonah 4:11 that God is indeed concerned about animals!

The Israelites of the Old Testament were predominantly agrarian, and a verse like Deuteronomy 24:5 would have spoken directly to them about how to treat their animals. The Corinthians, by comparison, were urbanites. Thiselton notes, "*The core community and core tradition of the city culture*

12. Anthony C. Thiselton, *The First Epistle to the Corinthians: A Commentary on the Greek Text*, New International Greek Testament Commentary (Grand Rapids: Eerdmans, 2000), 686.

13. Thiselton, *First Epistle to the Corinthians*, 686–87, citing Richard B. Hays, *First Corinthians*, Interpretation: A Bible Commentary for Teaching and Preaching (Louisville: Westminster John Knox, 1997), 151.

were those of trade, business, and entrepreneurial pragmatism in the pursuit of success, even if some paid a heavy price for business failures or for the lack of the right contacts or the right opportunities."[14] Thus, what Paul does in 1 Corinthians 9 is bring Deuteronomy 25:4 into conversation with the trajectory of the Corinthians in the context of the topic he is discussing. This, I think, is an example of what I am proposing in this chapter.

I am not suggesting that animal rights were not a problem in Corinth. I'm sure they were. However, we are aware of how badly animals get treated in industrial agriculture today, and thus when we bring Deuteronomy 25:4 into conversation with our context(s), it may well yield a sermon on animal rights and our responsibilities in this respect. Here we see how attending to the discrete witness of a text may be fertile for preaching today. Although the story is not well known, the same group of the Clapham Sect that fought for the abolition of slavery fought for animal rights as well and ended up founding the Society for the Prevention of Cruelty to Animals.[15] Work remains to be done in this area today in our consumer cultures.

Conclusion

Johann Georg Hamann (1730–1788) is one of the least known and most significant Christian philosophers. He studied at Königsberg University and then worked for the firm of a friend. He was sent on a diplomatic mission to London that fell apart. With money running out and living a dissolute life, he bought a Bible and tried to read it but made little progress. Later he tried again and was thoroughly converted. Still in London, he wrote his *London Writings,* a kind of commentary on the Bible. Hamann returned to Germany where his firm welcomed him back but was deeply concerned about his conversion. In an effort to convert him back to Enlightenment thinking, they introduced him to a philosopher at Königsberg University, Immanuel Kant. Hamann helped Kant get his "First Critique" published, and he wrote a critique of it before it was published.

Hamann begins his *London Writings* with a note of astonishment: God an author, what condescension![16] Our privilege is to respond to God's

14. Thiselton, *First Epistle to the Corinthians,* 4.

15. See Craig G. Bartholomew, *Where Mortals Dwell: A Christian View of Place for Today* (Grand Rapids: Baker Academic, 2011).

16. Johann Georg Hamann, *London Writings: The Spiritual and Theological Journal of Johann Georg Hamann,* trans. John W. Kleinig (Evansville, IN: Ballast, 2021).

condescension by listening. Listening, as we have seen in this chapter, is no simple or passive task. However, it is essential if we are to hear God's Word today. The preacher in particular needs to hone the practices of listening in order that he or she may preach. This listening extends beyond the Bible to our context today, so the preacher may land the plane of the sermon amid the particular congregation he or she is called to serve. None of us are adequate to this task, and so even as we hone such practices, we do so on our knees, praying again and again *"Veni Creator Spiritus*—Come, Creator Spirit."

DISCUSSION QUESTIONS

1. What do we mean by the clarity of Scripture? Explain.
2. Why do we appoint pastors and teachers in churches?
3. Can you think of several ways in which your culture is different from those in which the Bible was written?
4. How can you deepen your knowledge of your culture?
5. How does John Stott's notion of double listening help us with listening to the Bible today?
6. What does it mean to hear the message of the Bible at the intersection of two trajectories? Explain with examples.

FURTHER READING

Bartholomew, Craig G. *Excellent Preaching: Proclaiming the Gospel in Its Context and Ours.* Bellingham, WA: Lexham, 2015.

Stott, John. *The Contemporary Christian: An Urgent Plea for Double Listening.* Leicester, UK: Inter-Varsity, 1992.

———. *I Believe in Preaching.* Revised edition. London: Hodder & Stoughton, 2014. See especially chapter 4.

Wright, Christopher J. H. *Sweeter Than Honey: Preaching the Old Testament.* Carlisle, UK: Langham Preaching Resources, 2015.

DEVOTIONAL EXERCISE ──────────────────────────────────────┐

1. God speaks to us today. Take five minutes to come to stillness before God, ready to listen.

2. Read the following passage through several times.

   > **Exodus 24:1–2, 9–11**
   > Then the LORD said to Moses, "Come up to the LORD, you and Aaron, Nadab and Abihu, and seventy of the elders of Israel. You are to worship at a distance, but Moses alone is to approach the LORD; the others must not come near. And the people may not come up with him." . . .
   >
   > Moses and Aaron, Nadab and Abihu, and the seventy elders of Israel went up and saw the God of Israel. Under his feet was something like a pavement made of lapis lazuli, as bright blue as the sky. But God did not raise his hand against these leaders of the Israelites; they saw God, and they ate and drank.

   Imagine yourself as one of the seventy elders. Explore this remarkable story through his eyes. How do you feel, what do you see, what can you smell?

   How does this story relate to us in act 5 of the great drama of the Bible?

3. Imagine sharing a meal with Jesus. Speak to him about anything that is on your mind.

4. Conclude your time with this prayer from Numbers 6:24–27:

   > The LORD bless you
   > 　　and keep you;
   > the LORD make his face shine on you
   > 　　and be gracious to you;
   > the LORD turn his face toward you
   > 　　and give you peace.

SUGGESTED ACTIVITIES ———————————————————————

1. Watch a film or theater production that is widely acclaimed. What is its message? How would you build a bridge between the Bible and the film or drama you watched?

2. Consult your favorite reliable news source. Identify two stories that catch your attention. How does the Bible connect with them?

9

A LITURGICAL HERMENEUTIC

In the next three chapters, we will outline three approaches to reading the Bible that in my view are at the heart of biblical interpretation:

- A liturgical hermeneutic
- An ethical hermeneutic
- A missional hermeneutic

In chapter 4 we discussed the three aspects of biblical texts—literary, historical, and kerygmatic—that must be attended to. The dominant one is the kerygmatic, and it opens out into these three major directions (liturgical, ethical, and missional), as you will see from the diagram below.

FIGURE 9.1

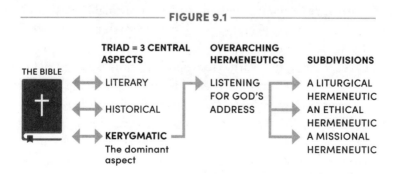

Listening to any biblical text yields at least three major questions:

- How is God offering himself to me/us through this text?
  (a liturgical hermeneutic)
- How is God instructing me/us about how to live?
  (an ethical hermeneutic)
- How is God equipping me/us for being sent into his world?
  (a missional hermeneutic)

As we will see, these three are closely related. Naturally, one will be more dominant in some texts than the others, but there is a logical order and primacy to these three questions, or hermeneutics.

Liturgical may strike some readers as strange, but I cannot think of a better word for what I have in mind here—though I make some alternative suggestions below. In more traditional churches, liturgy refers to what we do and the order in which we do it when we gather as Christians for worship. You do not need to be part of a traditional, liturgical church in order to understand this and make it your own. The way I am using *liturgical* applies as much to the gathering of a Pentecostal or an independent church as to a traditional Anglican one.

Whatever our style of doing church, the critical question is, Why do we gather? The order, form, style of music, and type of preaching vary tremendously from church to church, but we all need to answer the question of why we meet together. Of course, we gather for many reasons. For example, we gather for fellowship with one another, we gather to stay in touch with what is going on in our church, we gather in children's or adult Sunday school classes to be taught the Bible, and so on.

However, when we gather as a church for worship, there is surely one overwhelming reason why: to meet with God through Jesus and by the Spirit. The focus of true worship is not the leadership team or the band but the living God in our midst. We hear him address us through the reading and preaching of his Word. We respond in prayer and praise. In the Eucharist or communion, we share at his table, nourishing ourselves on Jesus, however exactly we understand the Eucharist as operating.

Liturgy is the means the Spirit loves to use to draw us yet again into the presence of the living God. The Word, the Bible, is at the heart of opening ourselves to the overwhelming reality of God who has come to us in Jesus by the Spirit. We may find ourselves asking, Is this really what the Bible is about, and if so, how do we read it in this way?

The Bible as Revelation

In chapter 3 we explored the concept of revelation, using categories from Christoph Schwöbel's excellent work on divine action and revelation. Revelation is all about God's disclosure of himself, and, of course, this far exceeds what we have in the Bible. God, for example, reveals himself in what he has made, in every aspect of his good creation. Theologians call this "general revelation." God can also speak directly to us or speak to us in dreams. Many missionaries have found, when they arrive to work among people who have never heard the gospel, that the Spirit has already been at work in dreams and other ways, preparing them to hear the good news of Jesus. The twentieth-century theologian Karl Barth observes that God is perfectly free to disclose himself as he wishes. God can speak to us through a dog, and if he does, we should listen. However, the authoritative place in which God speaks is the Bible, and it is the touchstone for all revelations of God.

The Bible tells the story of God's immersion in the life of ancient Israel and how it climaxes in Jesus, the Word become flesh. Sinai is the great mountaintop of the Old Testament, and you can read there how God revealed himself to the Israelites on Mount Sinai. Then, after the covenant was ratified, God had them build a portable, royal residence so he could dwell in their midst. This portable residence, the tabernacle, gives way to the temple once Israel is settled in the land. The temple is built by Solomon and indwelt by God.

The tabernacle and the temple are not just symbols of God's presence. God is actually and truly living among his people. This is what revelation and redemption are all about. Schwöbel says helpfully of God's self-giving that "God does not reveal propositions about God, God reveals himself."[1] Now, of course, in the process of God revealing himself we learn a lot about God. Exodus 34:6–7 is a great example of this: "And he passed in front of Moses, proclaiming, 'The LORD, the LORD, the compassionate and gracious God, slow to anger, abounding in love and faithfulness, maintaining love to thousands, and forgiving wickedness, rebellion and sin. Yet he does not leave the guilty unpunished; he punishes the children and their children for

---

1. Christoph Schwöbel, *God: Action and Revelation* (Kampen: Kok Pharos), 90.

the sin of the parents to the third and fourth generation.'" Widmer asserts, "Exodus 34:6–7 undoubtedly contains the most comprehensive account of YHWH's nature in the entire Bible."[2]

In his exploration of the attributes of God, the theologian William Abraham turns to Exodus 33:19 and 34:6–7. Abraham comments, "The initial predicates applied to God here are these: good, gracious, merciful, faithful, forgiving, and slow to anger. This suggests a cluster of attributes that we might more formally identify in and around the goodness of God."[3] He identifies the following cluster:

- God is all loving.
- God is the source of human flourishing.
- God is worthy of worship.
- God is just.
- God is holy.
- God is righteous, "intervening in history to fulfill his covenant promises, to put things right when they go wrong, and to vindicate those who put their trust in him."[4]
- God is free. "When God acts or engages in any activity, God freely and fully forms God's own intentions in such action or activity."[5]

Comparably, from Exodus 6:6–8 Abraham discerns the following attributes:

- God is all powerful.
- God is eternal and everlasting.
- God is all knowing.
- God is omnipresent.
- God is impassible.
- God is immutable.
- God's existence is necessary.

2. Michael Widmer, *Moses, God, and the Dynamics of Intercessory Prayer: A Study of Exodus 32–34 and Numbers 13–14*, Forschungen zum Alten Testament 8 (Tübingen: Mohr Siebeck, 2004), 169.
3. William Abraham, *Divine Agency and Divine Action*, vol. 3, *Systematic Theology* (Oxford: Oxford University Press, 2018), 57.
4. Abraham, *Divine Agency and Divine Action*, 3:57.
5. Abraham, *Divine Agency and Divine Action*, 3:58.

He asserts, "Taken together, lists like these begin to summarize the crucial ingredients that constitute a Christian doctrine of the attributes of God,"[6] and God's attributes reflect his nature accurately.

Clearly, there is a cognitive dimension to God's disclosure of himself. Some like to call this the propositional aspect of revelation. However, to reduce revelation to propositions is, as Vanhoozer points out, to catch only half the fish.[7] Revelation is a disclosure of God by God, and in the process what he offers as pure gift is . . . himself. God discloses himself in order that we might enter into relationship with him; knowing about God without knowing God himself is to miss the whole point of his self-disclosure.

Sinai and the Gift of God

You cannot read Exodus 19 without realizing that the theophany at Sinai is a self-disclosure by God to the assembled Israelites: "Then Moses led the people out of the camp to meet with God, and they stood at the foot of the mountain" (v. 17). And what a theophany and encounter it is! Fire, lightning, darkness, and an utterly overwhelming sense of the eternal, holy God. The Israelites are so filled with dread that they appeal to Moses to mediate between them and God. Until the covenant is ratified, the Israelites are in no position to experience communion with God.

However, as we noted earlier, once the covenant is ratified in Exodus 24, the most remarkable thing happens. The representatives of Israel ascend with Moses, see God, and enjoy a meal in his presence. This is the communion that the covenant is all about, the communion that is being opened to all the Israelites. When Moses stays on the mountain, he receives instructions for building God's royal, portable home, the tabernacle, so that God can literally dwell among his people from now on.

Having the living God in your midst is an immense challenge for sinful human beings. Thus, the cultus is established with the priests. Whereas in Egypt and other ancient Near Eastern cultures the priests were great landowners, in Israel the Levites did not receive their own part of the land as the other tribes had. They had one task: to mediate like a diplomatic corps between YHWH and his people, thereby maintaining the communion

6. Abraham, *Divine Agency and Divine Action*, 3:60.
7. Kevin J. Vanhoozer, *The Drama of Doctrine: A Canonical Linguistic Approach to Christian Theology* (Philadelphia: Westminster John Knox, 2004), 288.

between God and his people. This is what is at the heart of all those rites we read about in Leviticus.

Once Israel settled in the land, the temple was built under Solomon. From then on this was God's residence among his people. As one Jewish author reportedly put it, God now has an address on earth! God cannot, of course, be contained by a building, but his presence there is nevertheless literal and real. Pilgrimage to Jerusalem was mandatory for Israelites three times a year. They would cease their labors and journey to Jerusalem, where they spent time in God's presence and reimmersed themselves in the grand drama of which they were a part.

It is little wonder that in Exodus 19:4 God instructs Moses to tell the Israelites, "You yourselves have seen what I did to Egypt, and how I carried you on eagles' wings and brought you to myself." In ancient Egypt many of the great birds of prey were regarded as gods so that the Egyptian skies were full of their might. But YHWH, like a great eagle, has flown his people amid such powers out of Egypt on his back and "brought you to myself." This is the language of deep relationship, of communion, and it is at the heart of God's rescue of the Israelites and his self-revelation to them. At Sinai the gift that God offers is the gift of himself.

The great indicator of communion at the heart of the Old Testament is, of course, the Psalms, Israel's prayer book and hymnbook. You can learn a great deal about a people from their prayers and hymns. As discussed earlier, the Psalter is arranged in five books, deliberately mirroring the five books of the Pentateuch. If the Pentateuch is torah, God's instruction, the Psalms are the prayer and song book for a journey lived in response to God's instruction. And as we still discover today, communion with God is central to the Psalms.

The Christ Event and the Gift of God

In the New Testament, this personal and what I am calling liturgical dimension is ramped up to an entirely different level with the incarnation. This is perhaps nowhere more evident than in the Johannine literature.

John 1 tells us that in Jesus the Word (*logos*) became flesh and lived among us. In his extraordinary prologue, John reaches for a word that his Greek hearers would be familiar with: *logos*. In Greek philosophy the *logos* was the rational principle of the universe, and Greek hearers of John's prologue would have listened intently to hear what John had to say. Nothing would have prepared them for John saying that the *logos* became flesh. For the Greeks the *logos* was impersonal, whereas John proclaims a *logos* that is profoundly personal and becomes fully human.

What John does is take a word that his hearers were familiar with and fill it with Christian content. Understanding the deity of this *logos*, John recognized that the Word was responsible for the order in the creation, for apart from him nothing came into existence that has come into existence (John 1:3). However, for John, Jesus is the Word in a far richer sense than this. Words are the means by which we communicate with one another and, in deep relationships, the vehicles whereby we give ourselves to each other. It is this gift of self-disclosure that John has in mind when he calls Jesus the Logos, as we see in John 1:18. No one has ever seen God, but the only Son has made him known. We might more accurately translate this last phrase as "made available to be known," because it is quite clear from John's Gospel that it is not just knowledge about God but deep, personal encounter that John has in mind. If we wish to see and contemplate God, then it is Jesus we must focus on, and what an extraordinary picture of God emerges.

Another key difference between Greek thought and that of John's Gospel is the view of truth. For the Greeks truth was impersonal and referred to a correct understanding of the world. Truth is a major theme in John's Gospel, but truth is first of all a person—namely, Jesus. You will recall Jesus's statement "I am . . . the truth" (John 14:6).[8] Thus, for us ever to reduce the "truth" of the Bible to propositions, important as they are, is to lapse into a Greek worldview rather than the intensely personal biblical one.

Jesus is the one who takes away the sin of the world (John 1:29–34). He is the one who says to two of John the Baptist's disciples, "What do you want?" and then invites them to spend the day with him. He clears the temple because his "Father's house" has been transformed into a marketplace (2:13–22). He offers living water to the Samaritan woman at the well (4:7–26; cf. 7:37–39). He proclaims himself the bread of life (6:22–59). He does not condemn the woman caught in adultery (8:1–11). He proclaims

---

8. On truth in John's Gospel, see Craig G. Bartholomew, "The Spirit of Truth in John's Gospel and Biblical Hermeneutics," in *The Spirit Says: Inspiration and Interpretation in Israelite, Jewish, and Early Christian Texts*, ed. Ronald Herms, John R. Levison, and Archie T. Wright (Berlin: de Gruyter, 2021), 189–200.

himself the light of the world (8:12–20; cf. 1:8–9) and the good shepherd who knows his sheep and they him (chap. 10, esp. v. 14). He weeps over Lazarus's death and proclaims himself the resurrection and the life (chap. 11). He stoops to wash the feet of his disciples (13:1–20). He promises to send the Spirit, prays for his disciples (chap. 17), dies and rises again, appears to his disciples, and restores Peter to his place of leadership (21:15–19).

It is in all of this and far more (cf. John 21:25) that we are granted through Jesus the privilege to see and know God. It is truly an extraordinary and profoundly personal picture. Evangelicals are sometimes known for preferring the "meat" of letters like Romans, whereas Catholics tend to focus more on the Gospels. Of course, we need both, but for those of us who have believed in Jesus and received eternal life (3:16), we will want to linger long over the four Gospels because it is Jesus who shows God to us so that we might know him.

"Eternal life" is a favorite expression of John's and deserves close attention. Unlike the Synoptic Gospels, John rarely uses the language of the kingdom of God. But he has his own equivalent vocabulary, and eternal life is central to it. Eternal life is far too commonly understood as life in heaven forever, with the emphasis on *forever*. Years ago when I read the commentary on John by the great Anglican exegete Leon Morris,[9] I came to understand that this is inaccurate at best.

To understand eternal life, we have to grasp Jewish and biblical eschatology, where eternal life is not life in heaven but the life of the age to come. And for both Jews and Christians, this age to come is in history and not in heaven. The telos of the biblical story is not disembodied spirits in heaven but the resurrection of body and soul in the context of the new heavens and the new earth. The end of Revelation speaks eloquently to this. We do not go up to heaven, but heaven descends to the new earth, where God dwells with his people (Rev. 21–22).

Where Jewish and Christian eschatologies differ is in the belief that eternal life, the life of the age to come, is already in our midst, having begun with the coming of Jesus as recorded in the New Testament. And so the church, as Lesslie Newbigin so wonderfully puts it, is called to be a sign of the kingdom. Act 5 is the age of eternal life, the time between the coming of the King and the final consummation of the kingdom. The disciple of

9. Leon Morris, *The Gospel according to John*, rev. ed., New International Commentary on the New Testament (Grand Rapids: Eerdmans, 1995).

Jesus is one who already participates in the life of the age to come. If you have not understood this before, or even if you have, I encourage you to read through John's Gospel with this fresh understanding of eternal life. You will find it wonderfully illuminating.

And what, we might well wonder, does this eternal life look like? There are many answers to this question—answers like a renewed creation, a new creation, and so on. However, in his great high priestly prayer in John 17, Jesus captures the essence of eternal life in this statement: "Now this is eternal life: that they know you, the only true God, and Jesus Christ, whom you have sent" (v. 3). It is knowledge of this God who has come to us in Jesus that is at the very heart of eternal life.

It bears repeating that knowing God is not just knowing about God. In the Old Testament, "to know" can be a metaphor for sexual intercourse, thus evoking deep, intimate, personal knowledge. And it is such deep knowledge that Jesus has in view here. We see this repeatedly in John's Gospel but perhaps most clearly in John 14:23: "Jesus replied, 'Anyone who loves me will obey my teaching. My Father will love them, and we will come to them and make our home with them.'" This verse occurs in a section about the sending of the Spirit and is thus deeply trinitarian. But note the effect of loving Jesus and obeying his teaching: we will be loved by the Father (cf. Mark 1:11), and the Father and the Son will come and set up home with us. This is amazing, and it is hard to think of a more beautiful image for what eternal life is about than God setting up home with us. Perhaps my liturgical hermeneutic would better be called a domestic hermeneutic, a hermeneutic of the home. In the Old Testament, the tabernacle and the temple have the furnishings of a royal home. Here, in his condescension, God moves in with us.

It should be noted just what good news this is. Far from eternal life "just" being about the salvation of our souls, it is about the life of the age to come, the life in which all the brokenness of our own lives and the world is healed, and the creation is taken forward to that destiny for which God always intended it. In Christ we already participate in that life and the healing it brings. And that healing is holistic. We are relational creatures and made above all else for God. But when our relationship with God is broken, all our other relationships become fractured—our relationships with one another, our relationship with ourselves, and our relationship with the world. The really good news is that when we believe in Jesus and receive

---

eternal life, not only are we restored to God but the Spirit gets to work in our lives restoring all dimensions of our relationality. Irenaeus's words as they are commonly rendered express this wonderfully: "the glory of God is the human person fully alive."[10] Fully alive—this is what should happen when we listen to the Bible.

There is so much more to say. Before we move on, I must linger with Revelation 3:20: "Here I am! I stand at the door and knock. If anyone hears my voice and opens the door, I will come in and eat with that person, and they with me." The book of Revelation is a much-expanded letter or series of letters to the churches of Asia Minor, depicted as lampstands that hold forth the light and among whom Christ walks (Rev. 1:12–20). The depiction of Christ as the Son of Man is overwhelming and causes John to collapse at his feet as though dead. It is this same Son of Man who rebukes the church at Laodicea as neither hot nor cold and threatens to spit them out of his mouth (Rev. 3:14–22). Utterly remarkably, it is this very same Son of Man who speaks the words of Revelation 3:20. What grace, what condescension!

You may know the famous painting by William Holman Hunt, *The Light of the World*, depicting this scene or a comparable one. An original is housed at Keble College in Oxford in the chapel. Hunt's painting does not capture the vision of Christ in Revelation 1:12–16, but it does capture the image of Jesus knocking on the door of our lives. Whether intentional or not, the door has no handle on the outside but, presumably, only on the inside. We need to open the door.

Here is another possible name for our liturgical hermeneutic: the hermeneutic of the open door. Consider what happens when we open the door. We share an intimate meal with the Son of Man. Extraordinary.

Every Generation Brought to Sinai and Jerusalem

It has been observed that such is the significance of Sinai in the Old Testament that each generation of Israelites needs to be brought before God at Sinai, as it were. I say "as it were" because, although pilgrimage was mandatory in the Old Testament, Sinai itself never became a pilgrimage site for the Israelites. How then were they to be brought to God at Sinai anew

---

10. Irenaeus, *Against Heresies* 4.20.7.

FIGURE 9.2 *The Light of the World* (1853) by William Holman Hunt, oil on canvas

in every generation? Precisely through the narrative of Sinai as we have it from Exodus 19 to Numbers 10:11. In other words the Sinai narrative is written in such a kerygmatic way as to enable it to be told and experienced afresh, so that it is as if each generation is brought to Sinai. Through the narrative God offers himself afresh to each generation.

Jerusalem did, of course, become a major pilgrimage site for Christians. However, for Christians the Christ event needs to become contemporaneous so that we, too, can find our way—like the first disciples—to the confession that Jesus is the Messiah; so that we, too, can love Jesus and obey his teaching so that the Father and the Son come and set up home with us. How does this occur? Through the apostolic testimony that underlies the whole New Testament. This is why in Acts 2:42 the first converts devoted themselves to the teaching of the apostles, because it was in and through such teaching that they received more, far more, of Jesus. The whole intent of the New Testament is that in and through its apostolic witness we, too, should receive more and more of Jesus.

In Luke 10:38–42, just before Jesus's teaching of the Lord's Prayer (11:1–4), we find the story of Mary and Martha. The sisters host Jesus, but Martha becomes upset with Mary and Jesus when she is left to do all the work. In exasperation she appeals to Jesus. "'Martha, Martha,' the Lord answered, 'you are worried and upset about many things, but few things are needed—or indeed only one. Mary has chosen what is better, and it will not be taken away from her'" (10:41–42).

To paraphrase Augustine on this passage, I know what Mary was doing; she was eating Jesus![11] Augustine here, of course, appeals to a Eucharistic metaphor. The point is that in life one thing is necessary: silent, close attention to Jesus. Here, perhaps, is another name for my liturgical hermeneutic: the hermeneutic of the one thing necessary.

Conclusion

The Bible is God's special revelation. In it God discloses himself and offers us the gift of himself. We have seen how this is true of both Old and New Testaments. Not surprisingly, this is a theme already in Genesis 2–3. It has often been noted how Eden is depicted in temple imagery. Karl Barth

11. Augustine, *Sermons on the New Testament* 54.

observes how the tree of life is a symbol of God as the coinhabitant in Eden. And, of course, in Genesis 3:8 we read, "Then the man and his wife heard the sound of the LORD God as he was walking in the garden in the cool of the day, and they hid from the LORD God among the trees of the garden." Presumably this was God's normal practice, but it shows us Eden—that great park of "delight"—as a place of regular, delightful encounter between God and the first couple. At the other bookend of the Bible, in Revelation 21:3–4, we read, "And I heard a loud voice from the throne saying, 'Look! God's dwelling place is now among the people, and he will dwell with them. They will be his people, and God himself will be with them and be their God. "He will wipe every tear from their eyes. There will be no more death" or mourning or crying or pain, for the old order of things has passed away'" (citing Isa. 25:8).

The intimate knowledge of God is like a great river that runs from Genesis all the way through the Bible, cascading into the great waterfall of Revelation.

It is surely, therefore, imperative that we listen to the Bible in such a way that again and again we receive the gift of God himself. I have called this a liturgical hermeneutic. Alternatively, we could call it a domestic hermeneutic, a hermeneutic of the open door, or a hermeneutic of the one thing necessary. Whatever we call it, it needs to always be foremost in our biblical interpretation.

This is the reason you find *lectio divina* exercises after each chapter in this book. Amid the thrill of academic discussion, they are designed to draw us back to what the Bible and biblical interpretation are really about. Academic study of the Bible is a gift, but one that can become so stimulating that it becomes an end in itself. We must never allow this to happen. A *lectio divina* reading—a homiletical reading—and an academic reading need each other, and one can always be a corrective to another. However, we make a major, very modern mistake if we think it is always the academic analysis that provides the corrective, as though rational analysis of the Bible is the most important thing we can do with it. Academic biblical interpretation, done well, can profoundly deepen our understanding of the Bible. We saw, for example, how helpful Thiselton's rigorous work on 1 Corinthians is in our exploration of Deuteronomy 25:4 in 1 Corinthians 9. However, academic work on the Bible must always be in the service of listening for God's address, that address through which God offers us the gift of himself.

For a long time, academic interpretation in the form of commentaries and articles has been separated from deep, personal appropriation of the Bible as God's Word to us. The genres tend to be published in very different types of books, and one gets the impression that the two are separate entities. Certainly, people believe that serious academic work on the Bible should be kept apart from devotion to God and not exercised in the overt service of such devotion. In my opinion this ought not to be so. Why is it not possible to develop commentaries that combine devotion with the most rigorous scholarship, all in the service of listening for God's address?

It is a sign of our unhealth that it is rare to find this sort of liturgical hermeneutic in books on biblical interpretation. All sorts of wonderful and important technical information is provided, but how can we attend to all this information without asking, To what end were all the years of training and hours of hard work? The end or telos of our reading, listening to, and preaching the Bible must be to enter ever more fully into the very life of God himself. Among the many challenges of modern biblical interpretation, we may need to follow the example of T. S. Eliot—that is, to return to our starting point so we can understand it more fully now. We need to remember where and why we first became interested in the Bible, to retrieve the desire and love of learning because it led to more of God. Then we must allow this desire for God through his Word to be rekindled—and then evermore permeate and penetrate our most rigorous scholarship.

The Welsh doctor and preacher Martyn Lloyd-Jones became a famous London preacher and preached verse by verse through Romans 1–8 over several years to great acclaim. In his book on preaching, he asks what kind of preaching he looks for. His answer: preaching that ushers us into the presence of God. Lloyd-Jones understood the telos of the Bible, and so must we.

Of the three hermeneutics described at the beginning of this chapter, this—the liturgical hermeneutic—is the first because it is the most important. It represents the one thing necessary. Of course, when God sets up home with us, he teaches us how to live so as to please him and thereby to become fully human. Liturgy leads to ethics; it cannot be otherwise. And when we live with God and begin to learn how to live, we will find ourselves sent like Jesus and the apostles and the early church. Thus, we now move on to an ethical hermeneutic and a missional hermeneutic, ever aware that central to living and being sent will be living ever more deeply into God through his Word.

DISCUSSION QUESTIONS

1. Having read this chapter, how do you understand a liturgical hermeneutic?
2. What other names do I suggest for such a reading of the Bible? Which do you prefer, or do you have your own suggestion?
3. How important is the difference between knowing about God and knowing him personally? Explain in relation to your own experience.
4. Has studying the Bible increased your personal knowledge of God? If not, why do you think this is the case?
5. Why is the liturgical approach to the Bible so exhilarating?
6. How does this approach help you to hold together devotional reading of the Bible and academic study of it?

FURTHER READING

Ellis, E. Earle. "The New Testament's Use of the Old Testament." In *Biblical Hermeneutics: A Comprehensive Introduction to Interpreting Scripture*, edited by Bruce Corley, Steve W. Lemke, and Grant I. Lovejoy, 72–89. 2nd ed. Nashville: Broadman & Holman, 2002. This chapter is by one of my favorite New Testament scholars and is exceptionally good on biblical eschatology and, thus, the nature of eternal life.

Magrassi, Mariano. *Praying the Bible: An Introduction to* Lectio Divina. Translated by Edward Hagman. Collegeville, MN: Liturgical Press, 1998. This is a truly exceptional book that deserves a slow, close read. You will return to it again and again!

DEVOTIONAL EXERCISE

1. Even as your mind may be buzzing with information, come to stillness before God. Breathe in, breathe out, and sink down from your mind into your heart. Take five minutes just to be still before God.

2. How are you feeling? You can be honest with God, who is more on
   your inside than you are. Name your feelings and offer them to God,
   remembering that you are deeply loved by him.

3. Read the story of Mary and Martha several times, slowly mulling it
   over like a piece of hard candy in your mouth.

   ### Luke 10:38–42
   As Jesus and his disciples were on their way, he came to a village
   where a woman named Martha opened her home to him. She
   had a sister called Mary, who sat at the Lord's feet listening to
   what he said. But Martha was distracted by all the preparations
   that had to be made. She came to him and asked, "Lord, don't
   you care that my sister has left me to do the work by myself? Tell
   her to help me!"

   "Martha, Martha," the Lord answered, "you are worried and
   upset about many things, but few things are needed—or indeed
   only one. Mary has chosen what is better, and it will not be taken
   away from her."

   Imagine yourself as Martha and explore the story from her perspective.
   What thoughts and feelings come to mind?

   Are there many things that you are worried about?

   Now imagine yourself as Mary, and do the same.

   What stands out to you most from this story?

4. Imagine Jesus sitting next to you, and discuss the story with him.

5. Take five minutes to savor being in his presence.

6. Conclude your time with this prayer:

   Lord, thank you for the joy and exhilaration of the gift of learning. Grant that it may emerge from and ever be in the service of
   the one thing necessary. Amen.

SUGGESTED ACTIVITIES ──

1. Reflect on times when you have experienced God giving himself to you through the Bible. Has academic study of the Bible enhanced this experience or diminished it? If it has diminished it, explore how this chapter and book can help to change that.

2. There are so many things that distract us from the one thing necessary. Identify obstacles in your life to such attention and plan changes so that you really do attend to the one thing necessary.

10

AN ETHICAL HERMENEUTIC

In our discussion of a liturgical hermeneutic, we saw that when God reveals himself, what he gives is—himself. It is impossible to receive the gift of God and remain the same. Indeed, when God gives himself to us, the last thing we desire is to remain as we are. In the opening chapter, we spoke of running the way of God's commands, and this is always the desire of a person who has encountered God. Once Moses encountered God at the burning bush, for example, nothing in his life was ever quite the same again. Instead of taking it upon himself to exercise justice as he had done (Exod. 2:11–13), now he had to learn the vital importance of societal law as opposed to Egypt in which Pharaoh was the absolute, divine ruler and fount of legal decisions. Instead of leading like Pharaoh, in whose household he had grown up, now he had to learn how to lead God's people so as to facilitate God's reign over them. And just as he was learning to live differently, simultaneously he had to help his fellow Israelites do the same.[1]

Like Moses, once the Israelites encountered God at Sinai, they could not carry on with life as before. The covenant they entered with God at Sinai is filled with instruction (*torah*) about how they must live as God's people and so fulfill their calling to be a royal priesthood and a holy nation (Exod. 19:5–6).

1. See Leon R. Kass's fine commentary for a rich discussion of such issues: *Founding God's Nation: Reading Exodus* (New Haven: Yale University Press, 2021).

And so it was with the disciples and with Paul. It is unimaginable that after encountering Jesus on the road to Damascus that Paul's life would not have done an about-face. The Gospels are full of instruction about how to live as a follower of Jesus. Think, for example, of the Sermon on the Mount, the longest recorded sermon of Jesus (Matt. 5–7). And in the letters in the New Testament, most of them written by Paul, a common characteristic is the move from teaching about all that God has done for us in Jesus to how then we should live in the light of God's grace. It is simply impossible to read the Bible without running into instruction for living—ethics—at nearly every point.

And so it is with us. As Paul explains in his epochal letter to the Romans, in light of all that God has done for us in Jesus (Rom. 1–11), the only adequate response is to present our bodies as living sacrifices (Rom. 12:1–2). "Bodies" refers to the totality of our embodied personhood. A "living sacrifice" is paradoxical. An animal can only be a sacrifice by dying. We are called to be the living dead! We are called to die to the old, false self and to take on the exhilarating task of arising to the new, true self. We simply cannot do this without changing how we live.

Not surprisingly, the Bible is replete with teaching about how to live— what we call ethics. Even in Eden the first couple received instructions about what to do and what not to do. There is an abundance of instruction at Sinai (Exod. 19–Num. 10), as the Israelites become one nation under God. The prophets keep calling Israel back to live according to God's ways, and the wisdom teachers provide instruction in how to live amid the messy realities of life. When we think about biblical ethics, we tend to concentrate on core passages like the Ten Commandments. While that's appropriate, the Old Testament instructs us how to live in many different ways—through narrative; through Wisdom literature like Proverbs, Job, and Ecclesiastes; through the searing indictments of the prophets; through the story of the prophet Jonah; and through Israel's prayers and songs.

The last item may surprise you. But prayers and hymns do many things: prayer may petition God, praise God, lament before God, be still and attentive in the presence of God, contemplate God. Prayer also forms us as it situates us before the living God in a particular way. This is especially true of the Old Testament hymnbook, the Psalms, so much so that one recent, excellent book on the Psalms is titled *A Theological Introduction to the Book of Psalms: The Psalms as Torah.*[2] *Torah* means instruction, and even as we pray and sing the psalms we are formed by them and instructed about God and his ways—and thus our ways—in his world.

Prayer and an Ethical Hermeneutic

Prayer is the primary way in which we relate to God. It is always a response to God's prior giving of himself, and because it is primarily in and through the Bible that God gives himself to us again and again, prayer and a liturgical hermeneutic are inseparable. Both lead inevitably to ethics. Let me explain how this works.

Openness and attentiveness to God—prayer—orient us to the world in a particular way and to the way we are to live in it. As O'Donovan notes, "Developed and self-conscious moral thinking begins and ends by calling on God."[3] Prayer and a liturgical hermeneutic—reading the Bible to receive God—are the matrix of ethics. As O'Donovan perceptively notes, the self of theological ethics is a praying self. For O'Donovan prayer is the basic act of Christian ethics, the primal form of moral thinking, the heart of moral teaching, embodied in the vocative "Father," with which the Lord's Prayer begins. If ethics is concerned with human agency, then "prayer is the form that thought takes when we understand that agency implies a relation to the government of the universe, at once cooperative and dependent. It is precisely as prayer that moral responsibility may be assumed."[4]

O'Donovan pays particular attention to the Lord's Prayer in the Sermon on the Mount. With others he notes that it lies right in the center of the Sermon, surrounded by moral teaching.[5] What are we to make of this careful positioning? It alerts us to the centrality of prayer for action and thus for ethics, and it does this in a variety of ways.

2. J. Clinton McCann, *A Theological Introduction to the Book of Psalms: The Psalms as Torah* (Nashville: Abingdon, 1993).

3. Oliver O'Donovan, *Self, World, and Time*, Ethics as Theology 1 (Grand Rapids: Eerdmans, 2013), 38.

4. O'Donovan, *Self, World, and Time*, 38–39.

5. Context is always important in biblical interpretation. Note, e.g., where Luke positions the Lord's Prayer in 11:1–4. It arises out of Jesus's own practice of prayer (11:1), is preceded by the Mary-Martha story about the one thing necessary, and is followed by teaching on perseverance in prayer.

"Heaven" is the correlate of earth (cf. Gen. 1:1), and if we wish to understand the latter, of which we are part as human agents, then we need to start with the former. The former—that is, God who dwells in heaven—is available to us through prayer. Christologically, "[Christ's] address to God as Father corresponded to his understanding of himself, and in summoning disciples to call God 'Father,' he invited them to enter the position before God which he claimed for himself. As we call God 'Abba! Father!' our agent-identity is united with that of the Son."[6]

The phrase "on earth as it is in heaven," according to O'Donovan, qualifies "your will be done" as well as the two preceding phrases: "hallowed be your name" and "your kingdom come." In this way the Lord's Prayer looks for the purposes for which the world was designed and created to come to fruition. In his earlier *Resurrection and Moral Order*, O'Donovan notes that "the very act of God which ushers in his kingdom is the resurrection of Christ from the dead, the reaffirmation of creation."[7] Ethics is thus integrally related to God's order for his creation, and it is therefore creation wide and comprehensive in its scope. As O'Donovan delightfully states, "If in calling on the name we assert our agency as grounded on the gift of the name, in praying for it to be hallowed *we pray for effective encounter with the Holy in all our living and acting.*"[8] Another way of putting this is to say that having encountered God, we seek to live all of our life *coram Deo*, before the face of God.

O'Donovan says:

At the very center of this text of moral teaching ([Matt.] 6:1–18) there is the teaching of a prayer—not only how to pray, that is, but what to pray. Precise words are prescribed. If we have understood the relation of prayer to moral thought [ethics], we shall not be surprised at this. That such words should be open to private and public elaboration (*economical* elaborations, if we take Jesus' warning seriously!), that they should generate noble liturgies and passionate private intercessions may be taken as a matter of course. Yet the words are not merely an outline, a set of heads of advice or agenda items. They are themselves a possession of irreplaceable importance in forming the "we," the community of moral practice.

6. Oliver O'Donovan, *Finding and Seeking*, Ethics as Theology 2 (Grand Rapids: Eerdmans, 2014), 12–13.
7. Oliver O'Donovan, *Resurrection and Moral Order* (Leicester, UK: Inter-Varsity, 1986), 15. This point is nuanced in his preface to the second edition.
8. O'Donovan, *Finding and Seeking*, 13. Emphasis added.

That is why they should be placed—the bare text without embroidery or expansion—at the core of every Christian liturgy.[9]

O'Donovan here makes an important point—namely, the formative nature of the Lord's Prayer. To pray it is to orient and reorient ourselves again and again rightly in relation to God, ourselves, and the world. We can see why O'Donovan would describe the Lord's Prayer and thus prayer as the center of ethics, the primal form of moral thinking, the heart of moral teaching. It is central because the trinitarian God is at the heart of everything and not least of ethics, and prayer refers to that fundamental way that we relate to this God. Indeed, the Lord's Prayer functions as a hermeneutic, a framework for ethics. Cognitively, it sets out the major elements of the framework within which to understand moral action—most basically, heaven and earth and ourselves as creaturely agents on earth—and affectively, it positions us within that framework as adopted children in a right relationship with God. What the Lord's Prayer does *intensively*, Scripture does *extensively* as a whole. The Lord's Prayer is designed, in line with Paul and Augustine (Rom. 13:14[10]), to enable us to clothe ourselves with Christ. Sadly, in nonliturgical churches the Lord's Prayer is often neglected, and in liturgical churches we rattle through it, missing its profoundly formative nature. Few things can help us retrieve an ethical reading of the Bible as much as a thoughtful recovery of the Lord's Prayer in our worship and devotions.

When, for example, we pray that God's name—his character—be hallowed, among other things we are praying that his character will be treated as special in our own lives. In the language of the New Testament, we are praying for our sanctification, our becoming holy. As O'Donovan's extensive discussion of sanctification shows, we should not underestimate the depths involved in such a move. He says of sanctification, "The Holy Spirit brings God's act in Christ into critical opposition to the false structured reality in which we live. At the same time and through the same act he calls into existence a new and truer structure for existence. He gives substance to the renewed creation in Christ, giving it a historical embodiment in present human decisions and actions, so that it becomes partly visible even before its final manifestation."[11] The Lord's Prayer positions us at the heart of such divine action.

9. O'Donovan, *Self, World, and Time*, 64.
10. This verse was at the heart of Augustine's conversion. See Augustine, *Confessions* 8.12.29.
11. O'Donovan, *Resurrection and Moral Order*, 104.

Creation and Ethics

In his *Resurrection and Moral Order*, O'Donovan develops a biblical framework within which to think about ethics. He rightly asserts that the resurrection of Jesus bodily from the dead is a profound reaffirmation of creation. Christ does not rise as a disembodied spirit but as fully embodied. Similarly, in the Apostles' Creed, Christians confess that we believe in the resurrection of the body and the soul. All of this reaffirms what we find in Genesis 1—namely, that the materiality and nature of the creation is very good. Thus, O'Donovan is correct to say that we do not therefore set kingdom ethics (the teaching of Jesus) against creation ethics.

What is creation ethics? A metaphor can help us here. If you are a carpenter, then you know well that wood has a grain, and the easiest way to work with wood is to work along the grain. Similarly, there is a grain to the creation, built into it by God, and we flourish as humans when we live according to the grain of creation.[12] For example, Genesis 2 is clear that God has made humans male and female—Karl Barth notes that we only ever encounter humans as one of these: "Men are simply male and female"[13]— and, as such, for lifelong marriage, for becoming one flesh. Marriage is designed by God for deep relationship, as the context for the full enjoyment of our sexuality, and as the nest for the birth and formation of children. We know well that many today disagree with this and think, for example, that sex should be freely enjoyed whenever and with whomever we desire as long as no one gets hurt. From a biblical perspective, this involves living against the grain of the creation and will not lead to flourishing.

The kingdom of God—the main theme of Jesus's teaching—is about the recovery of God's purposes for his creation and his leading the creation toward the destiny he always had in mind for it. Thus, it would be exceedingly odd if kingdom ethics was opposed to creation ethics—though a deficient doctrine of creation will skew a proper understanding of redemption and of ethics. Remember that in Genesis 2–3 we find an unusual name for God: YHWH Elohim. YHWH, the name particularly associated with

12. R. W. L. Moberly, *The God of the Old Testament: Encountering the Divine in Christian Scripture* (Grand Rapids: Baker Academic, 2020), 28, similarly says of wisdom in Proverbs that it calls us to live "in tune with the way the world really is."

13. Karl Barth, *Church Dogmatics*, vol. III/1, *The Doctrine of Creation*, trans. J. W. Edwards, O. Bussey, and H. Knight, ed. G. W. Bromiley and T. F. Torrance (Edinburgh: T&T Clark, 1958), 186.

the exodus and Sinai, is the God who rescues Israel from slavery in Egypt and brings it to himself (Exod. 19:3–6); he is the Redeemer, Savior God. Genesis 1:1–2:3 uses the name Elohim, and the unusual combination of names (YHWH Elohim) in Genesis 2–3 flags for the reader that YHWH, the Redeemer God *is* the Creator God. Indeed, even in Exodus 19:3–6, as God explains what he has done and Israel's vocation in the light of his action, he reminds the Israelites that "the whole earth is mine." A biblical ethic must take creation, the first act in the great drama of Scripture, with utmost seriousness. Creation is the stage for everything that follows, and failure at this point will inevitably skew our ethics.

Sinai and Ethics

It might seem from all we have said that biblical ethics is easy and straight-forward. Often it is! You do not need to engage in complex maneuvers to work out that murder is absolutely wrong (the Ten Commandments) or that God does not recommend adultery as a nice way to spice up a faltering marriage. Often the problem we have with the teaching of the Bible is not that we struggle to understand it but that we struggle to obey it.

Having said this, in practice we encounter numerous ethical issues in daily life that the Bible does not directly address. Technology and artificial intelligence come to mind. What are we to make of algorithms, which increasingly govern our lives? There is no proof text or definitive passage in the Bible to appeal to on this issue. Even when we may think applying the Bible to life today is straightforward, it often is not. Take politics, for example. The Bible has much to say about politics, but it knows nothing of democracy, and the nation-state is itself a modern development. Not surprisingly, then, O'Donovan writes in his *Desire of the Nations*—a political theology published in 1996—that, whereas the preacher may move from the Bible to how to respond to Iraq in thirty minutes, such a move may encompass a scholar's lifetime of research.[14]

Why is this the case? The major reason is that history is part of creation. As Genesis 1:1–2:3 makes clear, God not only creates place(s) but also time; hence the "and there was evening, and there was morning . . ." repeated throughout the opening creation story in the Bible. God's creation opens

14. Oliver O'Donovan, *The Desire of the Nations: Rediscovering the Roots of Political Theology* (Cambridge: Cambridge University Press, 1996).

out into time and thus history. Even before the fall, creation was dynamic, with God intending that it develop toward a goal. The fall profoundly affects life in the creation, but the geographical and historical dimensions of life as created remain. And how we live in obedience to God will look different at different points in history, complicated severely by sin. There will be major commonalities, to be sure, but there will also be significant differences. This makes ethics contextual and challenging.

God's revelation at Sinai provides an example. As we noted above, Sinai involves an avalanche of ethical instruction. The Israelites arrive at Sinai in Exodus 19 and only take leave of it in Numbers 10. Between these two chapters is an immense amount of instruction from God, including the Ten Commandments in Exodus 20, as God provides torah for the formation of this nation as his people. It is entirely appropriate to feel that we strike ethical gold at this point. Israel is to become an ancient Near Eastern example of a nation under God's reign. Cultic instruction—what we might call worship—forms a major part of this, but only a part. The cultus is where the Israelites engage directly, liturgically, with the living God in their midst, but they do so precisely so that they might obey him in all other areas of life.

Not surprisingly, we find instruction about all aspects of life: worship, family, sexuality, law, work and rest, food and economics, art, building, agriculture, how to treat animals, politics, nationhood, education, and so on. Being in covenant with the Lord means every aspect of life is to be lived in obedience to God. Most ancient Near Eastern peoples had laws, but the Old Testament is unique in its articulation of the core of law or ethics in the Ten Commandments (Exod. 20; Deut. 5). The pithy range of the Ten Commandments is remarkable. The commandments move from worship (commandments 1–3) to rest (including for animals and foreigners) and work, to how we relate to one another—forbidding murder, insisting on faithfulness in marriage, prohibiting stealing, insisting on truthful testimony in law courts—to curbing the sort of desire that leads backward into breaking all the previous nine commandments.

Nowadays the Ten Commandments are often thought of as killjoys. But they are quite the opposite. Philip Rieff points out that every society, if it is to survive, has "thou shalt nots" (Rieff calls them interdictives).[15] A

---

15. Philip Rieff, *My Life among the Deathworks: Illustrations of the Aesthetics of Authority*, ed. Kenneth S. Piver, Sacred Order/Social Order 1 (Charlottesville: University of Virginia Press, 2006).

society in which anything goes is not freedom but hell. We can only flourish when solid, life-giving boundaries are in place, and this is precisely what the Ten Commandments are intended to provide. Patrick Miller memorably describes them as the ethos of the good neighborhood.[16] Imagine living in a town where insatiable desire was under control; people told the truth in law courts; nobody ever stole so you never had to worry about locking doors; marital fidelity was a prime virtue; human life was sacred; work was prized but with a lovely balance between work, rest, and worship—in short, a community in which God was honored in all areas of life.

The last point should not be overlooked. Rieff notes that throughout history—until now—culture making has always been thought of as the translation of sacred (God's) order into social order, a marvelous description of ethics. For the first time in history, we in the West are trying to generate cultures and societies apart from sacred order. The result, in Rieff's chilling word, is *Deathworks*.

Nor should we overlook the profundity of the Ten Commandments. René Girard, in his epochal *I See Satan Fall like Lightning*, argues that in the tenth commandment we find something absolutely unique in ancient culture: the constraint of mimetic desire, which he sees as the root of societal violence.[17] Girard develops a complex theory of desire, according to which humans develop by copying others (mimesis). However, such mimesis easily becomes competitive and escalates into violence. He tracks how this unique concern of the final commandment is fulfilled in Jesus and subverts at its deepest point the conflagration of desire that so often erupts in violence in human societies. Think of the fact that nearly every day there is a mass shooting in the US, and you begin to see just how attractive this good neighborhood is.

As I write, the very democratic foundations of the US are under threat as the Big Lie continues to be perpetuated and spread by former president Donald Trump and far too many Republicans. With astonishing speed, the insurrection at the Capitol on January 6, 2021, has been subjected to revision as a mere tourist visit. *The Washington Post* reports that over the four years

16. Patrick D. Miller, *The Way of the Lord: Essays in Old Testament Theology* (Grand Rapids: Eerdmans, 2004), 51–67.
17. René Girard, *I See Satan Fall like Lightning*, trans. James G. Williams (New York: Orbis, 2001).

of his presidency, Trump made 30,573 false or misleading claims.[18] In a society that honored the ninth commandment, such behavior would be utterly rejected and abhorrent. The ninth commandment refers first to testimony in law courts, but this is not to say it condones lying in the rest of life. Its concern is with the use of words and their God-given capacity to convey truth.

Thus, when we come to Sinai, we have indeed struck ethical gold. The temptation, once we grasp this comprehensive and delightful vision of Sinai, is to think that we can simply apply the teaching of Sinai to today. Not so fast.

There have been those so impressed by the ethical gold of Sinai that they see the move for the teaching of Sinai to its application to our societies as direct and straightforward. Some reconstructionists have argued for this approach. However, it is seriously flawed for the following reasons:

- Israel is an ancient Near Eastern nation and bears all the marks of this. Its language is that of ancient Hebrew, a dead language only recently revived in a modified form by Israel. Its ethics make sense in the context of the ancient Near East, and while its distinctives are often most interesting, the commonality with the peoples of the ancient Near East must not be ignored.
- Old Testament Israel is a geopolitical nation, whereas the church in the New Testament is scattered among the nations.
- Old Testament Israel is a theocracy in covenant with God. The church is a theocracy, but the nations in which the church exists are not. In Old Testament Israel, for example, adultery merited the death penalty. So, too, did the worship of other gods. Such laws signal unequivocally God's opposition to adultery and idolatry, but who among us would want to move quickly to advocate the death penalty for such behavior in our societies today? Indeed, many would argue that the practice of the death penalty today is indefensible.

So, yes, with Sinai we strike ethical gold. But, no, the move from Sinai to today is often anything but straightforward. Not only do we live in very different times, but we also live in a different act in the drama of Scripture, coming after the fulfillment of the Old Testament in Jesus.

18. Glenn Kessler, Salvador Rizzo, and Meg Kelly, "Trump's False or Misleading Claims Total 30,573 over 4 Years," *Washington Post*, January 24, 2021, https://www.washingtonpost.com/politics/2021/01/24/trumps-false-or-misleading-claims-total-30573-over-four-years/.

Entering the Kingdom

We mentioned earlier the Gospels' delightful metaphor for becoming a follower of Jesus: entering the kingdom (e.g., Mark 9:47). Remember, too, that the kingdom of God is the main theme of Jesus's teaching during his public ministry. All Jews looked forward in one way or another to God's definitive intervention in history to conquer his enemies and establish his rule. Jesus claims that with his coming the kingdom of God has arrived. But he also teaches his disciples to pray for the coming of the kingdom: "Your kingdom come" (Luke 11:2). What is going on here?

The Jews expected a single, definitive coming of the kingdom of God, but God's kingdom in Jesus comes in two stages.[19] With Jesus the kingdom has arrived; in his life, death, resurrection, and ascension, God has broken into the world and secured victory over sin and death so that the Christ event is the pivotal event in history. However, God's kingdom will only be consummated when Christ comes again in glory. In his first coming, Jesus entered the world incognito, with his major mission to go to the cross and beyond. At his second coming, he will return in glory as judge and ruler so that every knee will bow and every tongue confess that he is Lord.

This in-between time is where we live, and it is the great time of mission in which the news of Jesus is to be spread among all nations, with all invited to enter the kingdom. God's people are no longer a nation but are now *ekklēsia* scattered among the nations. This, of course, has huge ethical implications. In the Letter to the Hebrews, the author sets out the different situation in which we find ourselves (12:18–29). In verses 18–21, he describes the Sinai event and tells readers, "You have not come" to that mountain. The time has changed. Instead, "You have come to Mount Zion, the city of the living God, the heavenly Jerusalem" (v. 22). The section ends by noting that "our 'God is a consuming fire'" (v. 29), a clear reference to God's revelation to Moses in the burning bush and to the Sinai event. This is highly instructive: God does not change, but the context in which we serve him does.

The explosion of good news in the Christ event changes how we relate to and are informed by the instruction that comes out of Sinai. Jesus explicitly says that he did not come to abolish the Law and the Prophets (the

---

19. See E. Earle Ellis, "The New Testament's Use of the Old Testament," in *Biblical Hermeneutics: A Comprehensive Introduction to Interpreting Scripture,* ed. Bruce Corley, Steve W. Lemke, and Grant I. Lovejoy, 2nd ed. (Nashville: Broadman & Holman, 2002), 72–89.

Old Testament) but to fulfill them (Matt. 5:17). It is not uncommon to find scholars arguing that Paul abrogates the law for Christians. This is a complex and major topic and one you do well to explore in a course on the theology of Paul. Verses like Romans 10:4, where Paul says Christ is the "end" of the law, crop up in such discussions. The Greek word is *telos*, and it can mean end but also goal, culmination (NIV). In my view, Paul is not abrogating the law for Christians but teasing out how it has functioned and continues to function. A major way to get at the ethical continuity and discontinuity between the Old Testament and the New is to consider the meaning of the word *fulfill*.

As Hebrews sets out gloriously, Jesus is our great high priest and the great, final, and complete sacrifice for the purification of sins, once and for all. This is one significant way in which Jesus fulfills the Old Testament, and it makes obsolete much of the cultic legislation stemming from Sinai. It is not that we no longer learn from it—of course we do—but we no longer receive such instruction in the same way the Israelites did.

Jesus also fulfills the Old Testament by opening his kingdom to all nations and by shattering the wall of division between Jew and gentile (Eph. 2:11–22). As a result, the mission of the early church spreads from Jerusalem to Judea to the ends of the earth, with churches planted across the Roman Empire and beyond and with Paul as the great apostle to the gentiles. What comes of this is that much of the other Old Testament instruction no longer applies in the same way as it did to the Israelites. Because the church is not a nation, we cannot, for example, think we have to set up cities of refuge or go to Jerusalem three times a year on pilgrimage. However, these laws can still teach us. The cities of refuge were a way to prevent rash, violent vengeance and ensure that justice prevailed. Pilgrimage in the Old Testament meant that you and your extended family stopped work and traveled to Jerusalem for a major feast, thereby reimmersing yourself in the major story of which you were part, and then returned home to live out of that story more fully on a day-to-day basis. Pilgrimage, while not commanded, remains a means of spiritual formation today.

The relationship we now have with Sinai has become complex. How do we negotiate that complexity while retaining all the ethical gold? It is helpful here to remember Tom Wright's proposal that we need to leverage all the clues we can from the different acts in the drama of the Bible. We might say the legislation from Sinai moves from being law to becoming vital and indispensable clues as we seek to live under God's reign as a sign of the kingdom in this in-between age. The person who has developed the most helpful model in this respect is Chris Wright.[20] Wright argues that we need to think of Old Testament Israel as a paradigm of life under God's reign. It is a model of such life at a particular time (BC) in a particular way—as a nation in covenant with God. Because YHWH is the Creator God, this paradigm runs along the grain of creation at that time and in that way. This opens up the way for us to take from Sinai all it offers as a paradigm that we can incarnate in our different time (AD) and in our different context, scattered among the nations. Wright has himself demonstrated how fertile this is in relation to the economic law stemming from Sinai.[21] He points out, for example, how Old Testament law, in comparison to ancient Near Eastern law, prioritizes people over property. We need to work to ensure that the same is true of law in our own cultures, bearing in mind that our own concept of law in the West is very different from that of the ancient Near East.

The New Testament writers are intensely aware of this shift and wrestle with it. James Dunn suggests that what Paul is doing in Romans 13:1–7 is wrestling with the role of government in the new situation in which Christians found themselves, no longer part of a national theocracy but scattered among the nations.

While we must retain the ethical gold of Sinai—not least because of its overt national and thus public dimensions, faith opening out on all areas of life—at the same time we must not so stress the continuity between the Old and New Testaments that we miss what's radically new in the New Testament. This can be summed up in one word: Christ. In Christ the kingdom has come; the Spirit was poured out at Pentecost, inaugurating the new age and the birth of the church; and as a result, the early converts devote themselves to the teaching of the apostles because it was therein they found Jesus and learned how to follow him (Acts 2:42). Not surprisingly, therefore, Paul describes the life of the Christian as "in Christ," something radically new and different. New Testament ethics is Christocentric in a way that Old Testament ethics is not and could not be, and this makes a huge difference.

Jesus fulfills the Old Testament by embodying its vision as the true and perfect human being. For the first time, we can see, feel, and touch

20. Christopher J. H. Wright, *Living as the People of God: The Relevance of Old Testament Ethics* (Leicester, UK: Inter-Varsity, 1984).
21. Christopher J. H. Wright, *God's People in God's Land: Family, Land, and Property in the Old Testament* (Grand Rapids: Eerdmans, 1990).

what true humanity looks like (1 John 1:1). Much of this is best captured in narrative, highlighting the ethical importance of the Gospels. In his fully human life, Jesus not only reveals the Father to us, but he reveals *us* to us, and we do well to take note. This is one reason the motif of the imitation of Christ looms large in the history of Christian ethical reflection. Apart from the Bible, the most read book on Christian spirituality is Thomas à Kempis's *The Imitation of Christ*. It remains a very useful work, though skewed at the outset by its dependence on Jerome's misguided reading of Ecclesiastes as teaching *contemptus mundi*, contempt of the world. Healthier treatments of this theme are found, for example, in the writings of Herman Bavinck.

But the intuition is right. Think of the Beatitudes ("Blessed are . . .") that begin the Sermon on the Mount. These are the characteristics of the citizens of the kingdom of God. But they are also a description of the character of the King of that kingdom—namely, Jesus. The motif of being "like God" goes all the way back to Genesis 1:26–28 and is clearly visible in the Ten Commandments, which has been described as a legal commentary on the name YHWH.[22] However, with the coming of Jesus, we have an exemplar of what it means to be fully human in an unprecedented way.

There is also something more interior, more personal, more relational about kingdom ethics. This is signaled by the outpouring of the Spirit and Peter's use of Joel's prophecy to explain what was happening at Pentecost to the crowds observing the early Christians speaking the news of Jesus in a variety of languages or tongues (Acts 2; cf. Joel 2:28–32). The Spirit is, as John tells us in his Gospel, the Spirit of Jesus. He indwells individual believers, opening them noetically and affectively to what God has done in Christ, thereby enabling participation in the very life of God. In the exquisite language of John, the Father and the Son come and set up home with the believer. It would be wrong to deny the real presence of the Spirit among the Old Testament people of God. The Psalms bear eloquent witness to a profound spirituality. Nevertheless, after Pentecost there is a newness to the presence of the Spirit and his activity in the life of believers, not least in empowering their witness. As we've already noted, Tom Wright gets at this radical newness of kingdom ethics in his observation that "the Old Testament has the authority that an earlier act of the play would have, no

---

22. André LaCocque and Paul Ricoeur, *Thinking Biblically: Exegetical and Hermeneutical Studies*, trans. David Pellauer (Chicago: University of Chicago Press, 1998), 320.

more, no less."[23] It is not the charter for the church in the same way as the New Testament.

With the coming of the Spirit, there is also greater freedom and responsibility. The people of God now live among the nations of the world, and it is there that they are to be salt and light. Geopolitical realities always impinged upon Israel because of its geographical position between Egypt and Mesopotamia. However, now God's people are immersed in a variety of geopolitical realities, where they are to work out their salvation with fear and trembling, enhancing the reputation of their King amid the political, economic, educational, and social realities in which they find themselves.

It is sometimes argued that whereas in the Old Testament *place* is material and thick—consider the theme of the land—in the New Testament, land and thus place are spiritualized. This is quite wrong. The *king*dom is about God's reign, but it is also about the realm over which he reigns, his king*dom*. The themes of place and land are not spiritualized but extended to include the whole creation and all nations. Kingdom ethics is not less but more comprehensive than that of Sinai.

Unapologetically Hard Work

One of the best ways to honor the Bible is to recognize its limits. If I were speaking, I would say, "Let me repeat that." It is a profound mistake to think that we honor the Bible as God's Word by seeking in it answers to every question we have. This is simply not what the Bible is for. The Bible does answer many of our questions, but at a deeper level it orients us to the world in a particular way, with the trinitarian God at the center. Another way of expressing this is to say that the Bible provides us with a worldview. It is normative for all of life—how could it not be when it introduces us to the Creator of all? But *how* it is normative for all of life in our time and place requires hard work and deep reflection. Inspiration and perspiration work together.

Theologically, special revelation (the Bible) and general revelation (the ways in which God and his ways are revealed in the world and in history) go hand in hand, and ethics requires rigorous attention to both. The Bible offers, for example, poignant and indispensable clues to healthy political

23. N. T. Wright, "How Can the Bible Be Authoritative?," *Vox Evangelica* 21 (1991): 7–32, https://ntwrightpage.com/2016/07/12/how-can-the-bible-be-authoritative/. Quotes that follow are taken from this article.

life, but in order to see how those might shape politics today, we need an intimate knowledge of the history of politics and government and the state of politics at present. Through the lens of Scripture, we need to study how politics operates in God's good but fallen world, and only then can we be in a position to bring the insights of the Bible to bear creatively and with nuance on our politics today.

Theological ethics will only be theological if Christ and thus the Bible are central to it. However, there are other indispensable components, including history, philosophy, theology, and contemporary cultural analysis. In Christ we affirm the priesthood and the prophethood of all believers, but this needs to be understood comprehensively and deeply. Then we can begin the hard work that must accompany an ethical hermeneutic of the Bible.

Conclusion

An ethical hermeneutic follows logically from a liturgical hermeneutic. When God reveals himself to us, he gives us himself. But such a gift means that our view of the world changes and our lives must change. An ethical hermeneutic explores how and in what direction they must change if we are to enhance the reputation in the world of the God who has come to us by the Spirit in Christ. An ethical hermeneutic matters because we need to know how to live if we are to flourish and honor God. The two go together. An ethical hermeneutic also matters because if we are to testify to what God has done in Christ, then the way we live is an important part of that witness and also provides the indispensable plausibility structure against which our words about Christ will resonate and insist on being heard. An ethical hermeneutic thus leads logically and inseparably to a missional hermeneutic, the subject of the next chapter.

DISCUSSION QUESTIONS

1. The Bible is full of instruction about how to live. Can you list examples of such material?
2. Do all of the Ten Commandments (Exod. 20; Deut. 5) apply directly to us as they did to the ancient Israelites? Explain.

3. Read Matthew 6. How does the Lord's Prayer relate to an ethical hermeneutic?

4. How do the Beatitudes in Matthew 5:3–12 relate to the image of God in Genesis 1:26–28? This is a hard question. Be sure to ask your professor or minister if you need help!

5. How is our situation in act 5 of the great drama of Scripture different from that of the Old Testament Israelites?

6. Does the Bible answer all our questions about how to live today? Explain.

FURTHER READING

Bartholomew, Craig G., and Robby Holt. "Prayer in/and the Drama of Redemption in Luke: Prayer and Exegetical Performance." In *Reading Luke: Interpretation, Reflection, Formation,* edited by Craig G. Bartholomew, Joel B. Green, and Anthony C. Thiselton, 350–75. Scripture and Hermeneutics Series 6. Grand Rapids: Zondervan Academic, 2005. This resource is particularly concerned with prayer and biblical interpretation.

O'Donovan, Oliver. *Resurrection and Moral Order: An Outline for Evangelical Ethics.* Leicester, UK: Inter-Varsity, 1986. Of O'Donovan's many works, this book is especially useful. See also his trilogy Ethics as Theology.

Wright, Christopher J. H. *Living as the People of God: The Relevance of Old Testament Ethics.* Leicester, UK: Inter-Varsity, 1984.

DEVOTIONAL EXERCISE

1. Take five minutes to come to stillness before God. Know that your Father is already waiting for you as you come to him.

2. Reflect on your relationship with God. How has it been? How is it presently? What do you desire it to be?

3. Read the Lord's Prayer several times:

   Matthew 6:9–13
   This, then, is how you should pray:
   "Our Father in heaven,

182

Listening to Scripture

> hallowed be your name,
> your kingdom come,
> your will be done,
>> on earth as it is in heaven.
> Give us today our daily bread.
> And forgive us our debts,
>> as we also have forgiven our debtors.
> And lead us not into temptation,
>> but deliver us from the evil one."

4. Take note of anything that captures your attention.

5. Imagine Jesus sitting next to you. Talk to him about your prayer life and what you can learn from his teaching.

6. Slowly and reflectively pray the Lord's Prayer.

7. Conclude your time with this prayer:

> And now may the grace of our Lord Jesus Christ, the love of God, and the fellowship of the Holy Spirit, be with us all, evermore.

SUGGESTED ACTIVITIES

1. Identify a current event that cries out for ethical insight. Discuss it with a group of friends and try to identify all the ingredients in the recipe, as it were, that are needed if you are to come to a biblical view of the event and how to respond to it.

2. With a group of friends, identify temptations that you face. Determine for each whether the Bible provides clear direction about it or whether it is something that requires hard thought.

11

A MISSIONAL HERMENEUTIC

When Jesus said on the cross, "It is finished," it was as though it had all just begun. This is certainly true of act 5 of the great drama of Scripture, the act in which we find ourselves. It is the era of mission par excellence. All four Gospels contain a version of the Great Commission:

- In Matthew, Jesus commands his disciples to go and make disciples of all nations (28:16–20).
- In Mark, Jesus says to his disciples, "Go into all the world and preach the gospel to all creation" (16:15).[1]
- In Luke, Jesus says to his disciples that "repentance for the forgiveness of sins will be preached in his name to all nations, beginning at Jerusalem. You are witnesses of these things" (24:47–48).
- In John, Jesus says to the disciples, "Peace be with you! As the Father has sent me, I am sending you" (20:21).

In the Nicene Creed, we confess our belief in one holy, catholic, and apostolic church. The church is apostolic in two ways. First, it is built on the testimony of the apostles that underlies the New Testament. Second, the church, like Jesus and the apostles, is sent. It is missional to its core,

1. Note that the authenticity of the ending of Mark's Gospel is contested.

called and sent to go and bear witness to the good news of Jesus throughout the world.

This sense of the whole church as sent and thus missional is well captured in the Manila Manifesto, which speaks of mission as the whole church taking the whole gospel to the whole world.[2] This rediscovery of the sent-ness of the church does not and should not detract from the vital importance of what has been traditionally referred to as missionary work. In this respect Mike Goheen helpfully distinguishes between mission and missions, with the latter referring to the typical cross-cultural work that missionaries engage in. He writes, "Missions is one aspect of the broader mission of the church. Thus, it is narrower and has a particular focus. That focus is to establish a witness to the gospel in places or among peoples where there is none or where it is very weak."[3] Seeing the whole church as missional does not downplay such endeavors but positions them as exemplary within the context of a whole church that is sent into the world to bear witness to Jesus and the kingdom of God.

The renewal of mission has alerted us unequivocally that while mission includes evangelism it is about far more than evangelism.[4] A major topic at the important Lausanne Congress in 1974 was the relationship between evangelism and sociopolitical involvement. Both were affirmed as vital to the mission of the church.[5] Afterward Billy Graham pushed for a singular emphasis on evangelism, which John Stott successfully opposed.[6] In terms of our threefold hermeneutic, learning how to live from God and through his Word is essential in all areas of life. Our witness to the world must be in deed as well as in word, and without lives that match our message, our

2. Manila Manifesto (Lausanne II, Second International Congress on World Evangelization, Manila, Philippines, July 1989), https://lausanne.org/content/manifesto/the-manila-manifesto. This definition seems to come originally from Stephen Neill, "The Missionary Movement and the Ecumenical Movement," in *History's Lessons for Tomorrow's Mission: Milestones in the History of Missionary Thinking* (Geneva: World's Student Christian Federation, 1960), 251. It was subsequently adopted by the World Council of Churches' Commission for World Mission and Evangelism in Mexico City.

3. Michael W. Goheen, *Introducing Christian Mission Today: Scripture, History, and Issues* (Downers Grove, IL: IVP Academic, 2014), 402.

4. See Christopher J. H. Wright, *The Mission of God: Unlocking the Bible's Grand Narrative* (London: Inter-Varsity, 2006), chap. 6 and all the chapters in part IV.

5. In my view, the way Lausanne poses the question is problematic. See Craig G. Bartholomew, *The Church in Society*, 2nd ed. (Cambridge: Kirby Laing Centre, 2022).

6. See Timothy Dudley-Smith, *John Stott: A Global Ministry* (Leicester, UK: Inter-Varsity, 2001).

words will fail since they will lack the necessary backdrop that gives them meaning and authenticity. What a missional hermeneutic helps us see is that an ethical hermeneutic will include a critical engagement with the idols of our day as we seek to learn how to live.

The letters in the New Testament emerged out of the mission of the early church and were written to equip the church for its mission. Thus, it should not be surprising—and indeed it is one of the most fertile areas in biblical studies today—that in recent years a missional hermeneutic for reading the Bible has emerged. Chris Wright is one of the advocates of such a hermeneutic and also one of its ablest practitioners. In his seminal *The Mission of God: Unlocking the Bible's Grand Narrative,* he argues that "a strong theology of the mission of God provides a fruitful hermeneutical framework within which to read the whole Bible."[7]

In the twentieth and twenty-first centuries, missiology has flourished as never before, thanks to the work of those such as the British missiologist Lesslie Newbigin (1909–1998), who spent most of his career in India working out how the gospel engaged Indian culture and then returned to the UK to embark on exceptionally rich years of "retirement," as he sought to show the West as the great mission field today. South Africa produced one of our greatest missiologists in David Bosch (1929–1992), under whom I studied during my first degree. It is instructive how this renaissance of missiology emerged to a significant extent out of Majority World contexts, which then rebounded on the West. This renaissance has led to profound explorations of the nature of mission and, in the process, to a missional hermeneutic for reading the Bible.

In one sense the missional hermeneutic has demonstrated its fertility in reading the Bible for the church today. In the works of authors like Chris Wright, Tom Wright, Michael Goheen, Joel Green, Dean Flemming, and many others, rich missional readings of Old and New Testament texts can be found.[8] Chris Wright has also argued for and demonstrated the potential of mission for a comprehensive biblical theology, foregrounding the grand narrative of the Bible and how it all fits together and relates to us today. From another angle, vigorous debates continue about the precise nature of mission and of a missional reading. In this chapter we do not want to get

7. Wright, *Mission of God,* 26.
8. See esp. the essays in Michael W. Goheen, ed., *Reading the Bible Missionally,* The Gospel and Our Culture Series (Grand Rapids: Eerdmans, 2016).

into the weeds of such debates, important as they are. We will begin with the main characteristics of a missional hermeneutic and then situate my approach within that discussion before moving on to creative examples of this hermeneutic in action.

Characteristics of a Missional Hermeneutic

In an important article, George Hunsberger identifies the following major characteristics of a missional hermeneutic for the Bible.[9]

The Missional Direction of the Biblical Story

The overarching framework for biblical interpretation is the story the Bible tells of God's mission—the *missio Dei*—and God's formation of a people to participate in it. Wright's *The Mission of God* is the major example of this element. In contrast with my introduction to this chapter, Wright resists making "sent" central to "missional" and argues instead that "purpose" best defines what it is about.

Clearly, God had a purpose in his creation of the world, and this purpose became redemptive after the fall. God's purpose is to recover his original intent for the creation and to lead it toward the destiny he always desired. A people is central to this *missio Dei*. God's response to the avalanche of sin in Genesis 3–11 is to call one man, Abraham, and promise him that through him God would bless all nations, language that is synonymous with God's original purpose of blessing.

It is often debated whether the Old Testament can and should be read missionally. Clearly, Old Testament Israel is not sent into the world in the same way the early church is sent. However, once we relocate mission in God's purpose (with Wright), we can see that God's journey with Israel is always aimed at securing blessing for all nations through his people. Indeed, at the heart of the Sinai covenant, God has Moses tell the people, "Although the whole earth is mine, you will be for me a kingdom of priests and a holy

9. I am indebted for the shape of the material below to Christopher J. H. Wright, "Mission and Old Testament Interpretation," in *Hearing the Old Testament: Listening for God's Address*, ed. Craig G. Bartholomew and David J. H. Beldman (Grand Rapids: Eerdmans, 2012), 180–203. Wright, in turn, leans on George R. Hunsberger's "Proposals for a Missional Hermeneutic: Mapping the Conversation" (presented at the annual meeting of the American Academy of Religion / Society of Biblical Literature, 2008).

nation" (Exod. 19:5–6). In this remarkable text, the universal and the particular are both in view. Israel—the particular—is chosen by God to be his people. But the whole earth belongs to this God—the universal—and the Israelites are called to be a kingdom of priests and a holy nation amid the nations.

In Israel the priests mediated between God and the Israelites. Here the whole nation is called to mediate God's presence among all the nations. Thus, we can and should expect the writings of the Old Testament to have as a major goal equipping the Israelites for this calling so that they can participate in God's great mission. In this sense the Old Testament writings call for a missional reading.

Focusing on the purpose of God in this way opens up the great story of the Bible that moves from Genesis to Revelation. We have noted elsewhere how the Bible itself provides a framework for understanding the world and ourselves, and here in a related way we see how the unlocking of the grand narrative, to allude to Wright's work, provides a framework within which to read the Bible as a whole, asking of every part how it relates to God's overarching purpose of bringing blessing to the nations.

The Missional Purpose of the Writings

Chris Wright comments, as many of us who studied theology at mainstream universities have experienced, that when he read theology at Cambridge, his studies and his interest in mission seemed worlds apart. This is a sign of the dysfunction of much modern theology and biblical studies. Here, however, in a missional hermeneutic we find an approach that helpfully brings the two together again.

A missional hermeneutic argues that the biblical writings were written to equip God's people for their missional calling, and we ought to read them in this way for the church today. As already noted, this is clearly the case with the letters of the New Testament. As we will see below, missional readings of the Gospels have also proved fertile. Darrell Guder applies this approach to the documents of the New Testament,[10] and Michael Barram applies it to Paul's letters.[11] But what of the Old Testament? Chris Wright

10. Darrell Guder, "Biblical Formation and Discipleship," in *Treasure in Clay Jars: Patterns in Missional Faithfulness*, ed. Lois Y. Barrett et al., The Gospel and Our Culture Series (Grand Rapids: Eerdmans, 2004), 59–73.
11. Michael Barram, *Mission and Moral Reflection in Paul*, Studies in Biblical Literature 75 (Berlin: Peter Lang, 2005).

specialized in a study of Old Testament law, and he rightly argues that the laws of the Old Testament are given to form God's people into that holy nation and royal priesthood referred to above, precisely so that they can mediate God's presence to the world. Once we locate "missional" in "purpose" rather than "sent," we can see how not just the legal literature but all the books of the Old Testament are designed in this way and thus are part of a missional reading.

The Missional Locatedness of the Readers

Third, we have noted repeatedly in previous chapters that in order to listen to Scripture we have to allow it to penetrate our concrete reality. But what is the nature of our concrete reality? According to the biblical story, we are in act 5, the era of mission. This is above all else where we are located, and thus if we are to read the Bible faithfully, we have to read it from and in relation to this location. Hence the imperative for a missional reading.

Chris Wright develops this argument further, saying that mission is integral to the development and formation of the canon of the Bible. The literature of the Bible comes into existence precisely to keep equipping God's people to play their role in the *missio Dei*. Thus, it is not just us in act 5 who are missionally located; so, too, were the first readers of the texts of both the Old and New Testaments. For example, a developing insight is just how much of the Old Testament emerges in dialogue with surrounding cultures. We saw this in Genesis 1, where the author intentionally engages with the creation stories of surrounding nations. In missiological language we might call this contextualization. Wright perceptively asserts:

This observation that the canon of Scripture, including the Old Testament, is missional in its origin (in the purpose of God), and in its formation (in the multiple contexts of cultural engagement), means that so-called contextualization is not something we add to "the real meaning" of biblical texts, but is intrinsic to them. The task of recontextualizing the word of God is a missional project that has its basis in Scripture itself and has been part of the mission of God's people all through the centuries of their existence. The finality of the canon refers to the completion of God's work of revelation and redemption, not to a foreclosure on the necessary continuation of the inculturated witness to that completed work in every culture.[12]

12. Wright, "Mission and Old Testament Interpretation," 188.

The Missional Engagement with Cultures

According to a missional hermeneutic, the good news of Jesus, the gospel, functions as the interpretive matrix within which the Bible is brought into critical interaction with particular cultures and human contexts. Brownson shows how New Testament authors use Old Testament texts to help them grapple with relating the gospel to their context.[13] Indeed, recent studies of topics such as empire and Paul[14] and Revelation's critique of the Roman Empire[15] demonstrate unequivocally how the writers of the New Testament bring the gospel into critical dialogue with their surrounding cultures—and especially the Greco-Roman culture.

This is true of both the New Testament letters and the Gospels. In the Gospels we especially see the early church's critical engagement with Jewish culture. Jews had the Hebrew Bible and initiated the Greek translation of it (the Septuagint), but they understood its story as developing in very different ways from that of the Christians. Thus, right on their surface, the Gospels engage critically with their culture, telling the biblical story and its fulfillment against the backdrop of different Jewish perspectives of the day.

The One and the Three

There can be no question of the rich creativity that has been unleashed by missional readings of the Bible. To mention just one insight, a missional reading clearly subverts a Western individualistic reading of the Bible, for it is never just the individual but always the community that is sent. As illustrated in a previous chapter, my individualist reading of putting on the armor of God was neither true to the text of Ephesian 6 nor helpful to the hearers. Once the comprehensive scope of mission comes into view, it becomes clear that we can only engage in mission together. Indeed, we need to work together locally and across the globe. It comes as no surprise that Jesus, in his high priestly prayer in John 17, prays for the unity of his people.

13. James V. Brownson, *Speaking the Truth in Love: New Testament Resources for a Missional Hermeneutic* (Harrisburg, PA: Trinity Press International, 1998).
14. Richard A. Horsley, *You Shall Not Bow Down and Serve Them: The Political Economic Projects of Jesus and Paul* (Eugene, OR: Cascade, 2021).
15. Richard Bauckham, *The Climax of Prophecy: Studies on the Book of Revelation* (London: T&T Clark, 1993).

Undoubtedly, missional reading is a line of interpretation that must continue to be pursued. ~~But is a~~ missional hermeneutic *the* hermeneutic for reading the Bible? Readers of *The Mission of God* get the sense that for Wright it is. However, in their contribution to *A Manifesto for Theological Interpretation* on mission, Wright and Goheen back off from arguing that a missional hermeneutic is comprehensive, without indicating what it does not cover.[16] In the actual manifesto, they write: "On the one hand, mission is an essential hermeneutical key to reading the whole of Scripture. Mission is not just one of the many subjects that the Bible talks about. Rather, it is a way of reading the whole of Scripture with mission as a central concern. On the other hand, it is not the only lens employed to read the entire canon of Scripture since mission does not constitute the comprehensive subject matter of the biblical narrative."[17]

Perhaps it is not so much a question of what it does not cover as where its emphasis lies. Stephen Neill said that "if everything is mission, nothing is mission."[18] Is this a danger with a missional hermeneutic?

I am not sure. However, it seems to me best to position a missional hermeneutic as one major way of interpretation among the three we've discussed: liturgical, ethical, and missional. Undoubtedly these three overlap with each other—as we saw with regard to an ethical hermeneutic above—but there seems to me to be value in distinguishing them as I have done. As also discussed, they yield three major questions with every biblical text:

- How is God offering himself to me/us through this text?
- How is God instructing me/us about how to live?
- How is God equipping me/us for being sent into his world?

We will say more about the interrelationship of these three in the conclusion below. For now we will look at two missional readings, one from the Old Testament and one from the New.

16. Michael W. Goheen and Christopher J. H. Wright, "Mission and Theological Interpretation," in *A Manifesto for Theological Interpretation*, ed. Craig G. Bartholomew and Heath A. Thomas (Grand Rapids: Baker Academic, 2016), 172.

17. "A Manifesto for Theological Interpretation," in *A Manifesto for Theological Interpretation*, ed. Craig G. Bartholomew and Heath A. Thomas (Grand Rapids: Baker Academic, 2016), 15. See also my chapter, "Theological Interpretation and a Missional Hermeneutic," in Goheen, *Reading the Bible Missionally*, 68–85.

18. Stephen Neill, *Creative Tension: The Duff Lectures, 1958* (London: Edinburgh House, 1959), 81.

A Missional Reading of Jeremiah

Jeremiah has not always been well served by commentators, but it is one of my favorite books, not least because of the so-called prayers of Jeremiah, which give the reader unique access into a prophet's inner life. Wonderfully, in the middle of his chapter on "Mission and the Old Testament," Chris Wright maps out a missional reading of this book.[19]

Wright notes first that there are a surprising number of ways in which the issues the book of Jeremiah raises connect with our own:

- international turmoil, with the collapse of the brutal Assyrian Empire, the emergence of the Babylonian Empire, and the uncertainty of the future
- religious dysfunction among the people of God, with King Josiah's positive reformation but lingering idolatry and unhelpful nationalism
- the presence of terrible injustice and social evils
- the misuse of political power to quell dissent, including the murder of prophets and the agony experienced by Jeremiah
- the misuse of religious power with false prophets and corrupt priests
- the critical affirmation of God's sovereignty amid events that appeared to spell the end of Israel
- the ongoing mission of God's people even amid catastrophe
- grace and hope in the end

We noted in chapter 7 the importance of attending to the discrete witness of the Bible, and Wright notes that in this respect we need to take account of what Jeremiah's prophecies would have meant when spoken to those heading to exile, as well as what his book would have meant to those in exile. Psalm 137 gives us a sense of just how despondent the Israelites must have felt in Babylon:

> for there our captors asked us for songs,
> our tormentors demanded songs of joy;
> they said, "Sing us one of the songs of Zion!"

19. For his fuller treatment, see Christopher J. H. Wright, *The Message of Jeremiah: Against Wind and Tide*, The Bible Speaks Today (Downers Grove, IL: IVP Academic, 2014).

> How can we sing the songs of the LORD
> while in a foreign land? (vv. 3–4)

In this context Jeremiah 29:1–23 is a truly remarkable letter from Jeremiah to the exiles. In it God exhorts the exiles to build houses, plant gardens, and marry and have families. God's exhortation reaches a climax in verse 7: "Also, seek the peace and prosperity of the city to which I have carried you into exile. Pray to the LORD for it, because if it prospers, you too will prosper." "Peace" is the Hebrew word *shalom*, which evokes far more than a good feeling. It speaks of wholeness and order.

Wright comments that this exhortation gives the exiles a new perspective, a new mission, and a new hope. Amid a civic religion that falsely imagined that because of the temple YHWH was irrevocably committed to the land no matter how the people lived, exile would have come as a devastating shock to many Israelites. In the context of the loss of the land, prophets like Jeremiah played a crucial role, assuring the Israelites that God was still in control and not bound by the borders of the land of Israel. By continuing to speak through his prophets, YHWH brought new perspective and hope to his people. However, verse 7 calls them to a new mission even in this context, turning, as Wright says, their mourning to mission. They are to seek the welfare of Babylon, build houses, plant gardens, and have families. A remarkable exhortation!

As Wright observes, one can read the whole of Jeremiah through such a lens, asking what it would have meant to the exiles in their tragic situation of judgment and their new mission: "The so-called 'Book of Consolation' (chs. 30–33) would enable them to see that the promise of restoration for Israel would ultimately extend the knowledge of God among the nations, so that the hope of God for his people first expressed in 13:11, but so sadly frustrated by their sin, would eventually be fulfilled."[20]

As I complete this chapter, I find Wright's missional reading of Jeremiah compelling and encouraging. Here in Europe we have come staggering out of the pandemic into Russia's invasion of Ukraine, the first war on European soil since World War II. It is tempting to feel despondent with so much uncertainty and death. Liturgically, Jeremiah's prayers work well in this situation, and his call to a new mission amid God's sovereignty over what

---

20. Wright, "Mission and Old Testament Interpretation,"190.

seems out of control echoes deeply within my heart. In his extraordinary history of the city in the West, Lewis Mumford says that when the Roman Empire fell, the solution was already waiting in the wings.[21] For decades, indeed centuries, it had been quietly lived by the monks in the monasteries. Their positive influence was soon felt in the reconstruction of Europe, the abolition of slavery, the building of hospitals and poorhouses, as well as vast architectural projects. This is akin to what we hear in Jeremiah. In the darkest hours, let us keep living the solution, confident that God's purposes with his creation will have the final word.

A Missional Reading of Luke

Jesus is the center of mission, and David Bosch identifies five characteristics of the "missionary thrust" of the person and work of Jesus that are found in all four Gospels:

- Jesus's all-inclusive mission to Israel
- Jesus's understanding of the kingdom of God as already and not yet
- Jesus's emphasis on the reign of God rather than the Torah as center for the people of God
- Jesus's calling of disciples who are to be part of his missionary activities
- Jesus's resurrection shaping the identity of the early church[22]

Bosch takes the view that Luke wrote his Gospel for gentile communities. One major way in which Luke flags his missional concern is by writing not one but two books. Mission is central to Acts, but the two books are a unity: geographically, redemptive-historically, and in terms of the Spirit. Jesus begins his mission with the coming of the Spirit (Luke 3:21–22), and the same is true of the early church on the day of Pentecost so that the mission of the early church is clearly an extension of Jesus's mission.

21. Lewis Mumford, *The City in History* (New York: Harcourt, 1961), 247.
22. David J. Bosch, *Transforming Mission: Paradigm Shifts in Theology of Mission*, 20th anniversary ed. (New York: Orbis, 2011). In this section I am drawing on the important chapter by Michael W. Goheen, "A Critical Examination of David Bosch's Missional Reading of Luke," in *Reading Luke: Interpretation, Reflection, Formation*, ed. Craig G. Bartholomew, Joel B. Green, and Anthony C. Thiselton, Scripture and Hermeneutics Series 6 (Grand Rapids: Zondervan Academic, 2005), 229–64.

A key text for Bosch is Luke 4:16–19, the Nazareth Manifesto. According to Bosch, in these verses Jesus proclaims a revolutionary and unique missionary program. Verses 18–19 are at the heart of this section:

> The Spirit of the Lord is on me,
>   because he has anointed me
>   to proclaim good news to the poor.
> He has sent me to proclaim freedom for the prisoners
>   and recovery of sight for the blind,
> to set the oppressed free,
>   to proclaim the year of the Lord's favor.

From the Nazareth Manifesto, Bosch identifies three major themes in Luke: the mission to the gentiles, the importance of the poor, and the putting aside of vengeance in favor of peacemaking. In the verses above, Jesus quotes the Servant Song in Isaiah 61:2, but he stops halfway through the verse and does not announce the day of vengeance. It was this omission that sparked opposition to Jesus. Although Jesus focuses his mission on the Jews, there are important signs already in his ministry of a move beyond to the gentiles; for example, the way in which he treats the Samaritans (Luke 9:51–56; 10:25–37; 17:11–19). In Luke's version of the Great Commission, the move beyond Israel becomes clear. The themes of salvation and repentance are central to Luke, and the Great Commission is expressed in these terms. Bosch is adamant that salvation in Luke cannot be reduced to one's vertical relationship with God. He quotes Scheffler, who identifies no less than six dimensions of salvation in Luke: economic, political, social, physical, psychological, and spiritual.[23] For Bosch, in mission the church is called to embody the kingdom of God.[24]

Bosch's reading is rich and insightful, as Goheen acknowledges. In his critique, however, Goheen cites Bosch's comparative neglect of the Old Testament. Bosch sees mission as the major difference between the Old Testament and the New. By comparison, Goheen, like Wright, stresses the continuity of the Bible in this regard. As Goheen points out, Luke him-

23. Eben Scheffler, "Suffering in Luke's Gospel" (PhD diss., University of Pretoria, 1988), 57–108. Published as *Suffering in Luke's Gospel*, Abhandlungen zur Theologie des Alten und Neuen Testaments (Zürich: Theologischer Verlag, 1993).

24. See Goheen, "Critical Examination," 253, for a list of nine characteristics of the sort of community envisaged from a missional reading of Luke.

self is at pains to make the connections between Israel's mission, Jesus's mission as the continuation and fulfillment of Israel's, and the church's mission as the continuation of Jesus's. Goheen asserts, "The connection can be made not only forward from Jesus' mission to the church's mission, but also back from Jesus' mission to Israel's mission. Not only does the church continue Jesus' mission, but Jesus fulfills Israel's mission. The Servant Songs of Isaiah must be put back in the context of the broader Old Testament story of a people called to incarnate as a community the redemptive purposes of God in the midst of the world for the sake of the nations."[25]

Goheen argues that there are other missional themes in Luke to which Bosch does not do justice, such as prayer, suffering, table fellowship, and the role of the Spirit. These are indeed major themes in Luke with important implications for mission. Luke has an unusual emphasis on prayer in his Gospel and mentions Jesus praying at virtually every crucial point in his ministry.[26] Suffering, too, is an important theme in relation to mission. Mike Goheen has often reminded me how mission goes forward invariably accompanied by suffering.

Conclusion

It will be apparent from this chapter that a missional reading is vital for the contemporary reception of the Bible. As we conclude I return to how the three major hermeneutics I have identified for biblical interpretation fit seamlessly together.

In the Bible, which is God's revelation, his Word written, God offers us nothing less than himself. Of course, he is God, and he never offers himself completely or in a way in which we possess him. Nevertheless, again and again as we attend to and listen to Scripture, God offers us the gift of himself; the Father and the Son, by the Spirit, want to move in with us, to set up home in our midst. This is extraordinary, and it is something we must never lose sight of, not least among churches that are often activistic

---

25. Goheen, "Critical Examination," 257.

26. See Craig G. Bartholomew, *Revealing the Heart of Prayer: The Gospel of Luke* (Bellingham, WA: Lexham, 2016); Craig G. Bartholomew and Robby Holt, "Prayer in/and the Drama of Redemption in Luke: Prayer and Exegetical Performance," in Bartholomew, Green, and Thiselton, *Reading Luke*, 350–75.

and so busy doing the "Lord's work" that they have no time for the Lord himself. Jesus began his ministry at the age of thirty; for most of his life he lived quietly as a carpenter. Even when he began his public ministry, he punctuated it regularly with time alone with God. We subvert the Bible if we do not read it as the means by which God gives himself to us again and again.

However, when the Father and the Son move in with us, our lives change. We learn how to live along the grain of the creation today, instructed by God through his Word. Scripture is normative for all of life, including ethics. Thus, it becomes our great joy to read the Bible with a view to being instructed how to live for God today. This is good news. Patrick Miller's description of the Ten Commandments as the ethos of the good neighborhood is apt. Who would not want to live in such a neighborhood? And as we learn the Messiah—as Ephesians 4:20 puts it—we discover that, far from such ethics distorting our humanity, truly the glory of God is the human person fully alive.

A liturgical hermeneutic carries with it spiritual formation; an ethical hermeneutic carries with it ethical formation. Both are absolutely essential for mission. A mistake we often make is that once we are converted we think we are ready to save the world. However, conversion is a starting point, and if we are to engage in mission we need to be *being* formed and *becoming* those who live out the gospel in daily life.

To be drawn into the life of God is to be drawn into his purposes. We must not make Peter's mistake of finding the revelation of Jesus so wonderful on the Mount of Transfiguration that he proposes staying there (see Luke 9:28–36). No, Jesus must descend in order to fulfill his mission of leading the whole creation in its exodus (Luke's word) from sin and death. Likewise, we will discover that even as we are drawn into the life of God and start to become like God in how we live—the *imago Dei*—we will also find ourselves sent out into the world to bear witness in word and deed to the overwhelming reality of this God who has come to us in Jesus. And a missional hermeneutic reminds us that a major role of the Bible is to equip us for that outward journey.

Take and read. Take and listen. A feast awaits.

DISCUSSION QUESTIONS

1. What is the difference between mission and missions? Why is this important?
2. What did this chapter identify as the main characteristics of a missional reading of the Bible?
3. Do you think mission is present in the Old Testament? Explain.
4. Using John's version of the Great Commission, can you explain how our being sent is similar to and different from that of Jesus?
5. What is the relationship between a missional hermeneutic and those that are liturgical and ethical?
6. How do you feel about being sent? Explain how this chapter informs your feelings.
7. Is it possible for a journalist, a lawyer, or a politician to be involved in mission? Explain.

FURTHER READING

Goheen, Michael W. *The Church and Its Vocation: Lesslie Newbigin's Missionary Ecclesiology*. Grand Rapids: Baker Academic, 2018.

———. *Introducing Christian Mission Today: Scripture, History, and Issues*. Downers Grove, IL: IVP Academic, 2014.

———, ed. *Reading the Bible Missionally*. The Gospel and Our Culture Series. Grand Rapids: Eerdmans, 2016.

Wright, Christopher J. H. "Mission and Old Testament Interpretation." In *Hearing the Old Testament: Listening for God's Address*, ed. Craig G. Bartholomew and David J. H. Beldman, 180–203. Grand Rapids: Eerdmans, 2012. Chris is one of a handful of authors about whom I tell my students, "Read everything he has written!"

———. *The Mission of God: Unlocking the Bible's Grand Narrative*. London: Inter-Varsity, 2006.

DEVOTIONAL EXERCISE

1. As we come to the end of our journey together, reflect for a moment on where we began—that is, the joy of running the way of God's instruction.

2. Take five minutes to come to stillness before God.

3. Reflect on the gift of God's Word. Remember his desire to give himself
   to you again and again. Take time to open your heart to God, ready to
   receive once again the gift of himself.

4. Read this passage from John several times, mulling it over in your heart.

   John 20:19–22
   On the evening of that first day of the week, when the disciples
   were together, with the doors locked for fear of the Jewish leaders, Jesus came and stood among them and said, "Peace be with
   you!" After he said this, he showed them his hands and side. The
   disciples were overjoyed when they saw the Lord.
   Again Jesus said, "Peace be with you! As the Father has sent
   me, I am sending you." And with that he breathed on them and
   said, "Receive the Holy Spirit."

   Imagine yourself as one of the disciples. See the scene through his
   eyes. What are you feeling, and what stands out for you?

   Focus on Jesus's words. How do they resonate with you?

5. As one who is sent just as Jesus was sent, imagine Jesus sitting next
   to you, and talk to him about this.

6. Conclude your time with this prayer:

   Father, thank you for the great gift of your Word. Help me attend
   to it in such a way that again and again I will receive the gift of
   yourself. Help me to hear your commission to me to go, even
   as Jesus was sent.
   Lord, in your mercy,
   Hear my prayer.

SUGGESTED ACTIVITIES

1. Meet with a missionary or invite one to address your class. Listen
   carefully to the missionary's story, and if possible, discuss how his

or her involvement in missions relates to the mission of the whole church.

2. Read one or more of the major statements about the mission of the church that have come out in recent decades—for example, the Lausanne Covenant or the Manila Manifesto.

SCRIPTURE INDEX

SUBJECT INDEX